AF576783

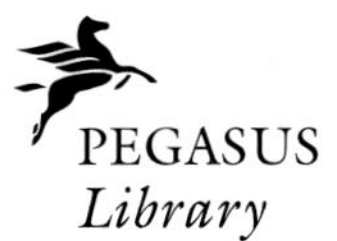
PEGASUS
Library

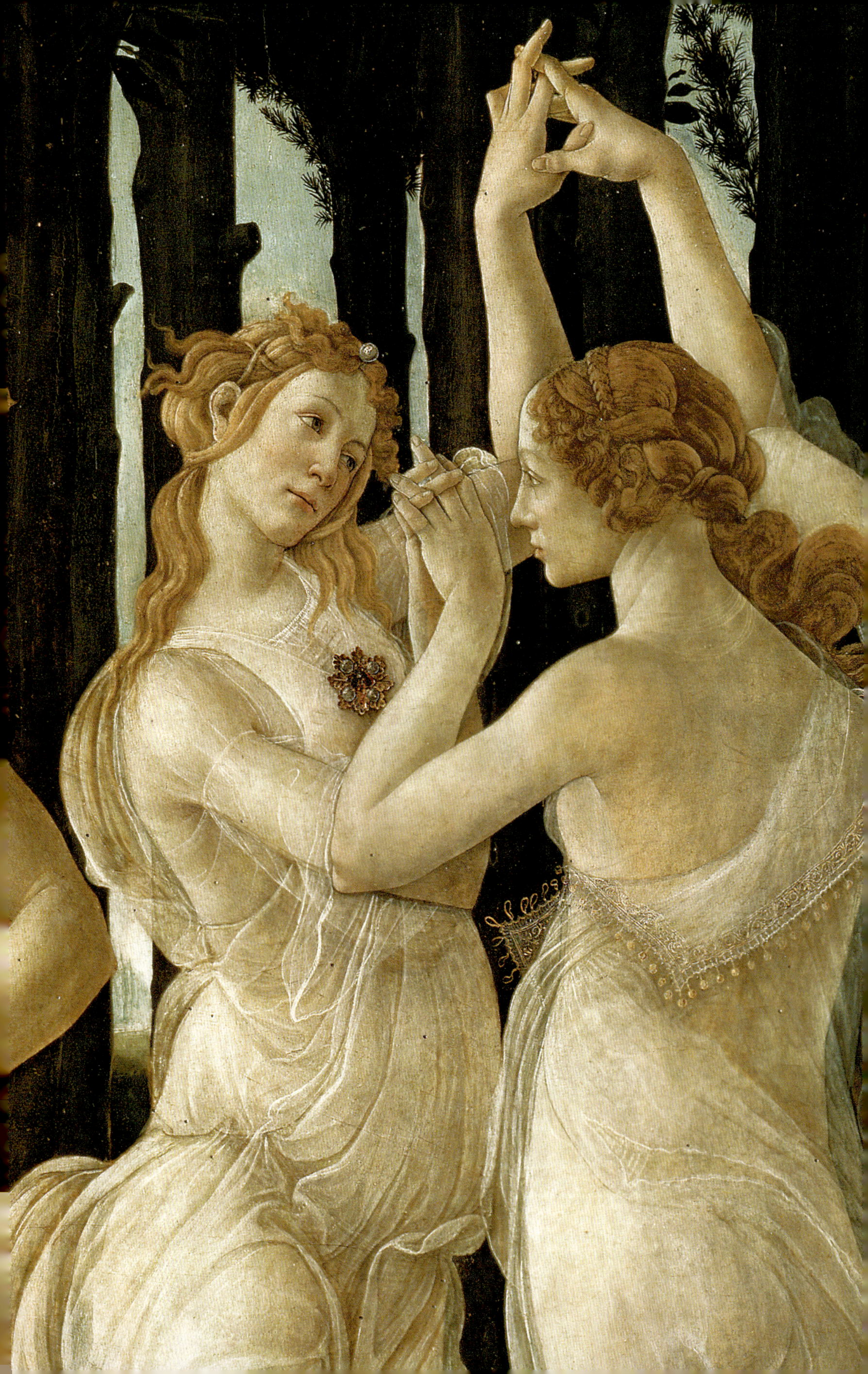

Frank Zöllner

BOTTICELLI

Images of Love and Spring

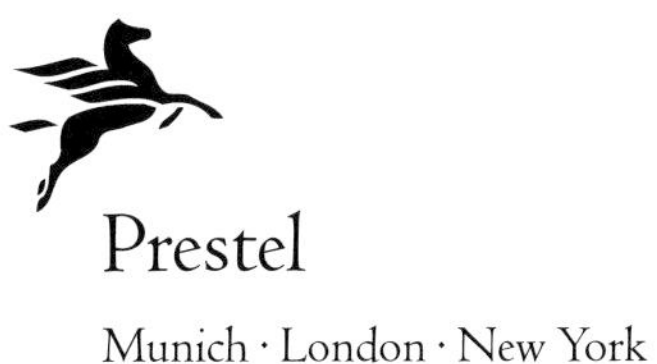

Prestel

Munich · London · New York

On the cover:

Front cover: *La Primavera* (detail), see pp. 32–33
Spine: *The Birth of Venus* (detail), see pp. 80–81
Frontispiece: *La Primavera* (detail), see pp. 32–33

Photography credits on p. 127

Mandlstrasse 26 · D-80802 Munich, Germany
Tel. +49 (89) 381709–0; Fax +49 (89) 381709–35
and 16 West 22nd Street, New York, NY 10010, USA
Tel. (212) 627–8199; Fax (212) 627–9866

Prestel books are available worldwide.
Please contact your nearest bookseller, or write to either
of the above addresses for information concerning your local distributor.

Translated from the German by Fiona Elliott
Edited by Jacqueline Guigui-Stolberg and Jane Milosch

Designed by Karin Mayer
Typesetting by Reinhard Amann, Aichstetten
Lithography by ReproLine, Munich
Printed by Passavia Druckservice GmbH, Passau
Bound by MIB Conzella, Pfarrkirchen

Printed in Germany on acid-free paper

ISBN 3–7913–1985–X (English edition)
ISBN 3–7913–2025–4 (German edition)

Contents

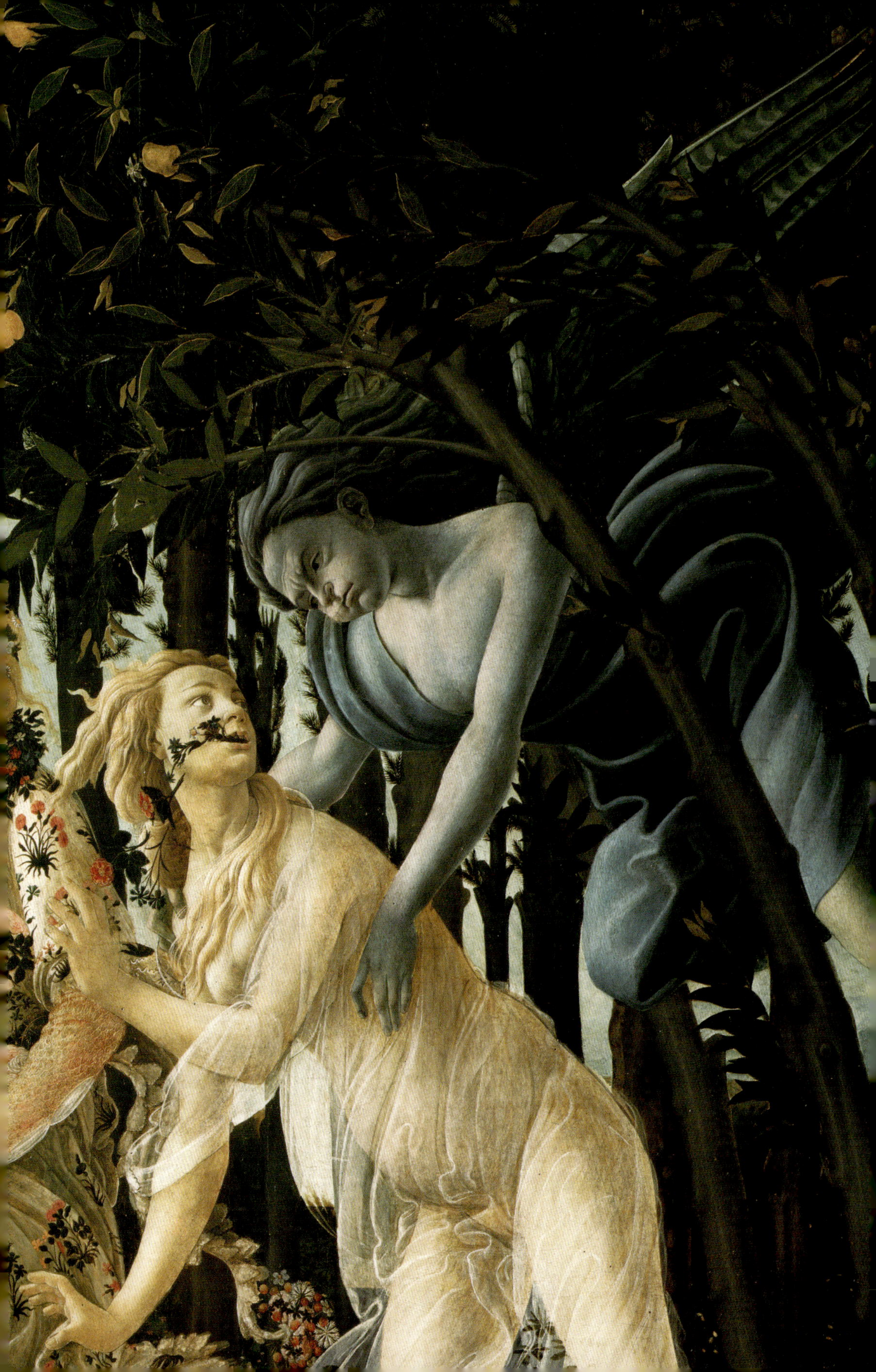

Myths and Mythological Pictures

In 1459, when Alessandro Filipepi was apprenticed to a goldsmith in his home town of Florence, he was a thirteen or fourteen-year-old boy from a humble background. He showed no exceptional gifts and soon abandoned the prestigious trade of goldsmith to train as a painter. At that time probably no one would have predicted that Sandro Botticelli, as he was known from then onwards, would become one of the most important painters of the fifteenth century. Yet within a few years Botticelli began to receive commissions from the patrician-connoisseur families of Florence and to create his large-scale depictions of scantily dressed gods and goddesses — the most extraordinary mythological paintings ever seen.[1]

The best known of Botticelli's mythological works are *La Primavera* and the so-called *Birth of Venus,* two works which secured his fame already in the sixteenth century and which — since his rediscovery in the nineteenth century — have come to be recognized as marking the climax of Florentine Renaissance painting. Botticelli's mythological paintings also include two medium-size works, *Minerva and the Centaur* and *Mars and Venus,* as well as the frescoes that were discovered in a Florentine villa in 1873 and which show a young man among the personifications of the Liberal Arts and a young woman with Venus and the Graces. It is these six works by Botticelli — their making and their meaning — that we will devote our attention to in *Images of Love and Spring.*

Chloris and Zephyrus, detail from *La Primavera,* c. 1482

In terms of their contents, these paintings by Botticelli take up tales from the pre-Christian mythology of classical antiquity which tell of the lives of gods and heroes, of their dealings with each other and with human beings.[2] Although the fabulous stories from the inexhaustible fund of ancient mythology were never entirely forgotten during the Middle Ages — indeed they were present in medieval manuscript illumination — before the fifteenth century it was relatively rare to find depictions of gods and heroes in large-format paintings. Similarly, it was unusual to find depictions of nude or barely dressed, life-size figures. It was only due to the flourishing of the literary arts in cities and towns, together with the renewed interest in classical texts and the revival of the visual arts in the fifteenth century, that painters once again turned to the legends of classical antiquity.[3]

The most significant, large-scale works which demonstrate the increasing importance of classical texts for fifteenth-century painting first emerged in the courts of northern Italy. A typical example of this new interest in the depiction of ancient gods can be seen in Francesco del Cossas's Salone dei Mesi (Hall of the Months) for the Palazzo Schifanoia in Ferrara;[4] these drew on the astrology and mythology of antiquity, linking the ancient planet-gods with the court of Duke Borso d'Este. During the same period, Andrea Mantegna's works for the court of the Gonzaga family in Mantua were positively alive with the forms and ideas of antiquity.[5] In the *camera picta* of the ducal palace, for example, Ludovico had the ceiling painted with a mythological fresco portraying his virtues as a ruler. Not long after this, Sandro Botticelli in Florence was painting his own mythological scenes, although not for a courtly patron, but for the wealthy and powerful bourgeois elite, among whom the Medici family was by far the most important.

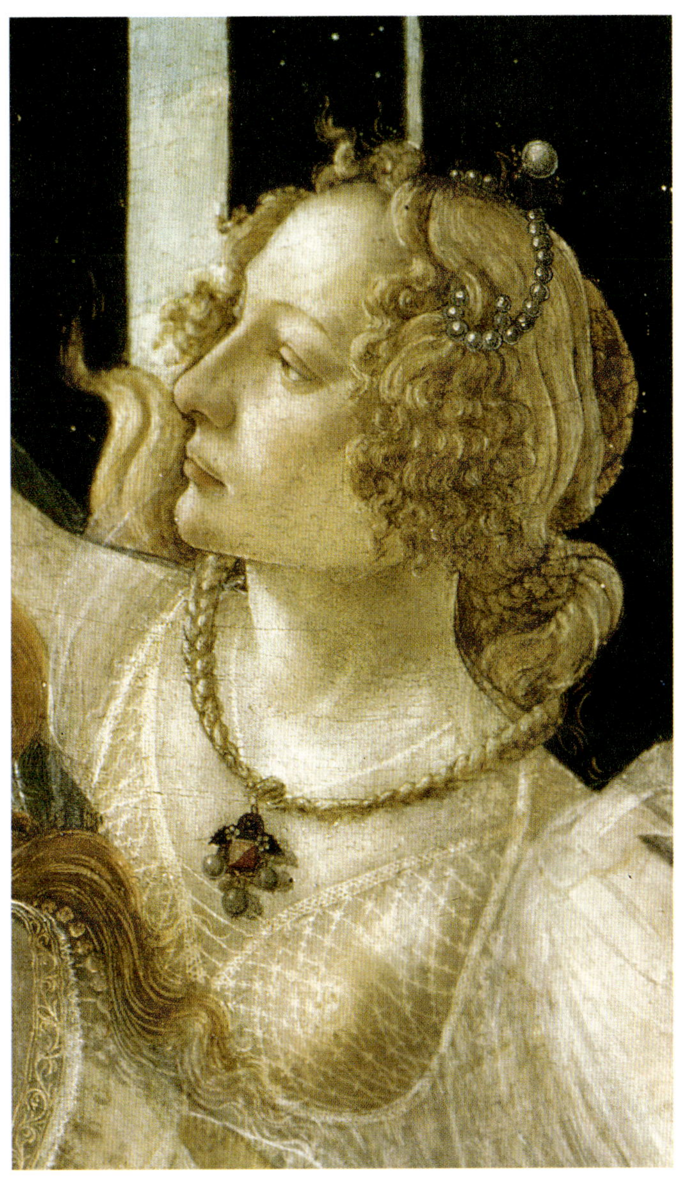

One of the Three Graces, detail from *La Primavera,* c. 1482

The myths and characters so richly described and illustrated in ancient sources served not only to enlighten and educate interested readers and viewers, but they also illustrated characters and patterns of behaviour (both exemplary and otherwise), and they invited responses and interpretations of all kinds. Above all in the period between the sixteenth and the nineteenth centuries, countless works with occasionally very complex mythological themes were created as models or reflections of individual and collective modes of behaviour corresponding to the demands and customs of both courtly and bourgeois circles. Classical mythology has largely lost the importance it once had, and we are only occasionally reminded in passing of its former status — as in the choice of the title *Pegasus* for this series of books. While implying certain qualities, this name is also open to interpretation: Pegasus is the winged steed of the Muses — the goddesses of poetry, the arts, and the sciences — and stands metaphorically for flights of artistic and poetic imagination. And it may well be that the publisher was hoping to encourage such flights of imagination in the authors and readers alike. Any reference to the winged horse of antiquity can precipitate a whole variety of allusions.

In the same way, Botticelli's mythological paintings — above all *La Primavera* and *The Birth of Venus* — have been interpreted over the years in a variety of ways. Most often they have been understood as representations of the philosophical principles of Florentine Neo-Platonism, which expressed a complex theory of love, or as responses to contemporary and classical texts.[6] Whatever the case, the general tenor of these interpretations is not always consistent with the factual circumstances of the making of these individual works. Therefore, in our discussion, there will be less talk of philosophical depths and philological heights than of the circumstances — fortunate and unfortunate — in the lives and loves of the addressees, and of the meaning that these works were to convey to the viewers at the time they were made.

The meaning of the sensual and yet strangely reticent figures in Botticelli's work may perhaps be best explained by Marsilio Ficino's words in a letter to Lorenzo il Magnifico de' Medici (Lorenzo the Magnificent): "Much do the philosophers argue, the orators declaim, the poets sing, in order to exhort man to a true love of virtue.... I think, however, that Virtue herself (if she can be placed before the eye) may serve much better as an exhortation than the words of men. It is useless to praise a girl in the ears of a boy, or describe her with words, if you want to arouse him to love.... Point, if you can, to the fair maiden herself with your finger and no further word will be needed. One cannot describe how much more easily the sight of Beauty inspires love than words can do. If, therefore, we could present the wonderful aspect of Virtue itself to the eyes of men there would no longer be any need for our art of persuasion."[7]

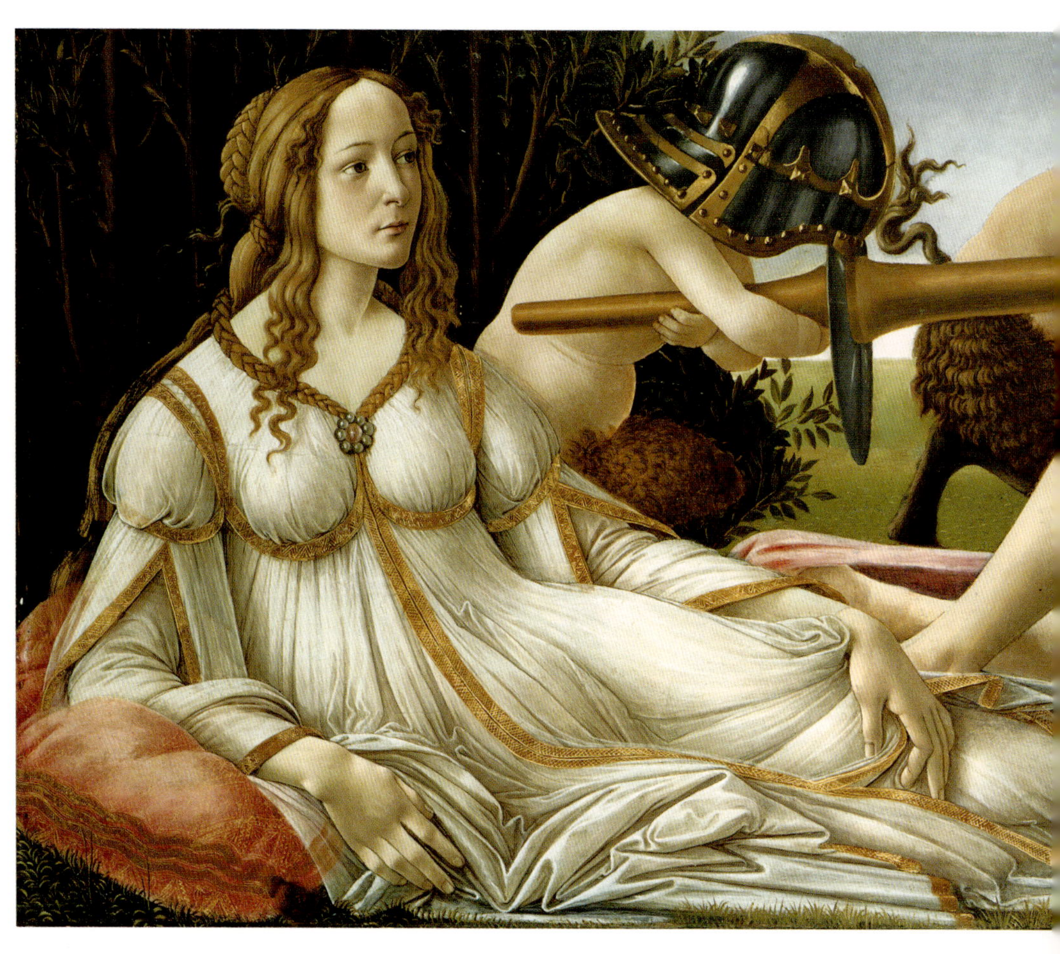

Mars and Venus, 1483

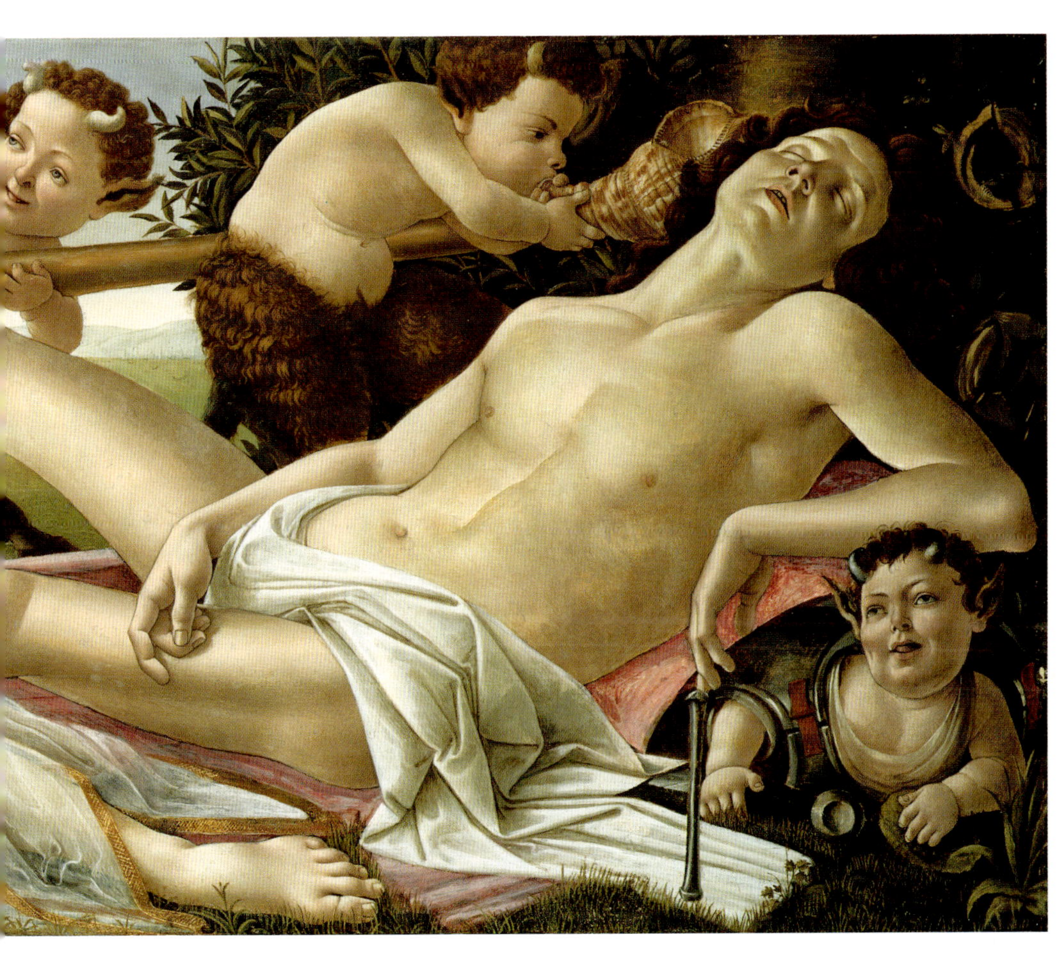

Mars and Venus: Forerunners and Sources in Antiquity

The gods and goddesses, like the heroes and heroines of classical antiquity, by no means always appear alone. The god finds his goddess or sometimes an earthly mortal, the hero finds his heroine. The characters in the mythology of the ancients frequently appear as couples, and their problematic relationships are the subject of many legends. Among the most prominent couples of antiquity are Mars and Venus along with Amor and Psyche (whose love stories end happily), Orpheus and Eurydice, and Apollo and Daphne (whose stories have less happy endings). Mars and Venus were *the* classical couple, as it were, portrayed together by Sandro Botticelli somewhere between 1480 and 1485.[8] Painted on wood and in an unusually long, horizontal format, this work is reminiscent of pictures that were made to decorate wedding chests. These chests, known as *cassoni,* were made throughout the fifteenth century for weddings and the subject matter depicted on them generally reflected this occasion. Botticelli's *Mars and Venus,* however, probably first served as a decorative painting within a *spalliera* (the wooden wall-panelling of a room). This type of painting was very popular at the time and was frequently commissioned to commemorate a marriage. It is also conceivable that this work was incorporated into the framework of a *lettuccio* (a large day bed), and thus was intended as a *lettuccio* painting (a decorative headboard to a day bed). Domenico Ghirlandaio's fresco, *The Birth of Mary,* in the church of Santa Maria Novella in Florence gives us an impression of what

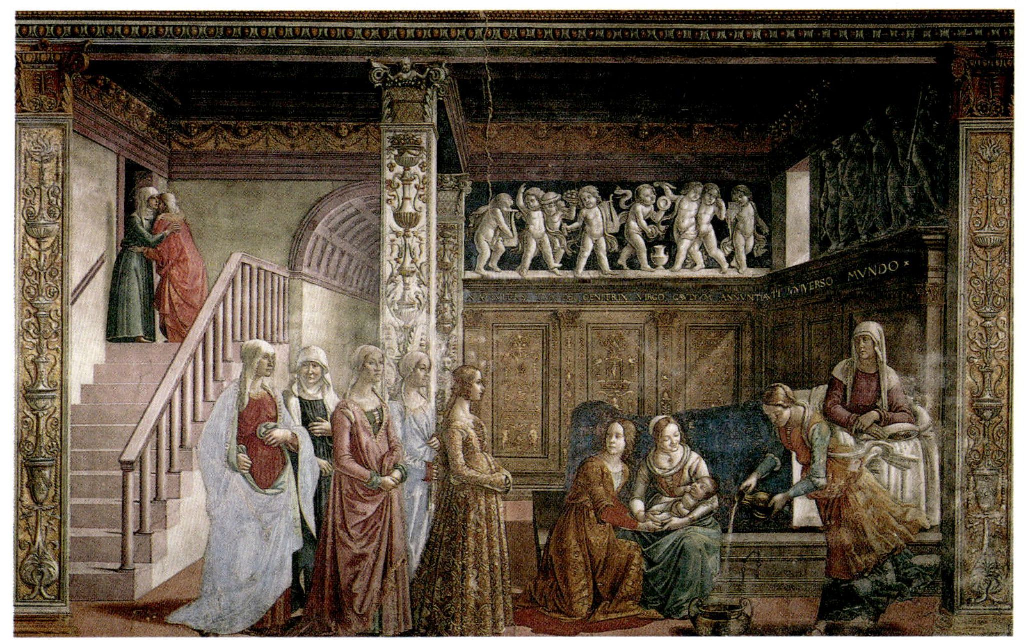

Domenico Ghirlandaio
The Birth of Mary,
c. 1485–90

these rooms must have looked like with his depiction of a *lettuccio,* of splendid marquetry within a *spalliera,* and of dancing putti in the *cornici* (moulding)[9]. Extravagant and colourful paintings could often be found instead of marquetry work or putti to enliven these panelled surfaces. Giorgio Vasari, in his *Lives of the Most Eminent Painters, Sculptors, and Architects* (first published in 1550), described the importance of these types of pictures: "the citizens of those times used to have in their apartments great wooden chests in the form of a sarcophagus, with the covers shaped in various fashions, and there were none that did not have the said chests painted; and beside the stories that were wrought on the front and on the ends, they used to have the arms, or rather, insignia of their houses painted on the corners, and sometimes elsewhere. And the stories that were wrought on the front were for the most part fables taken from Ovid and

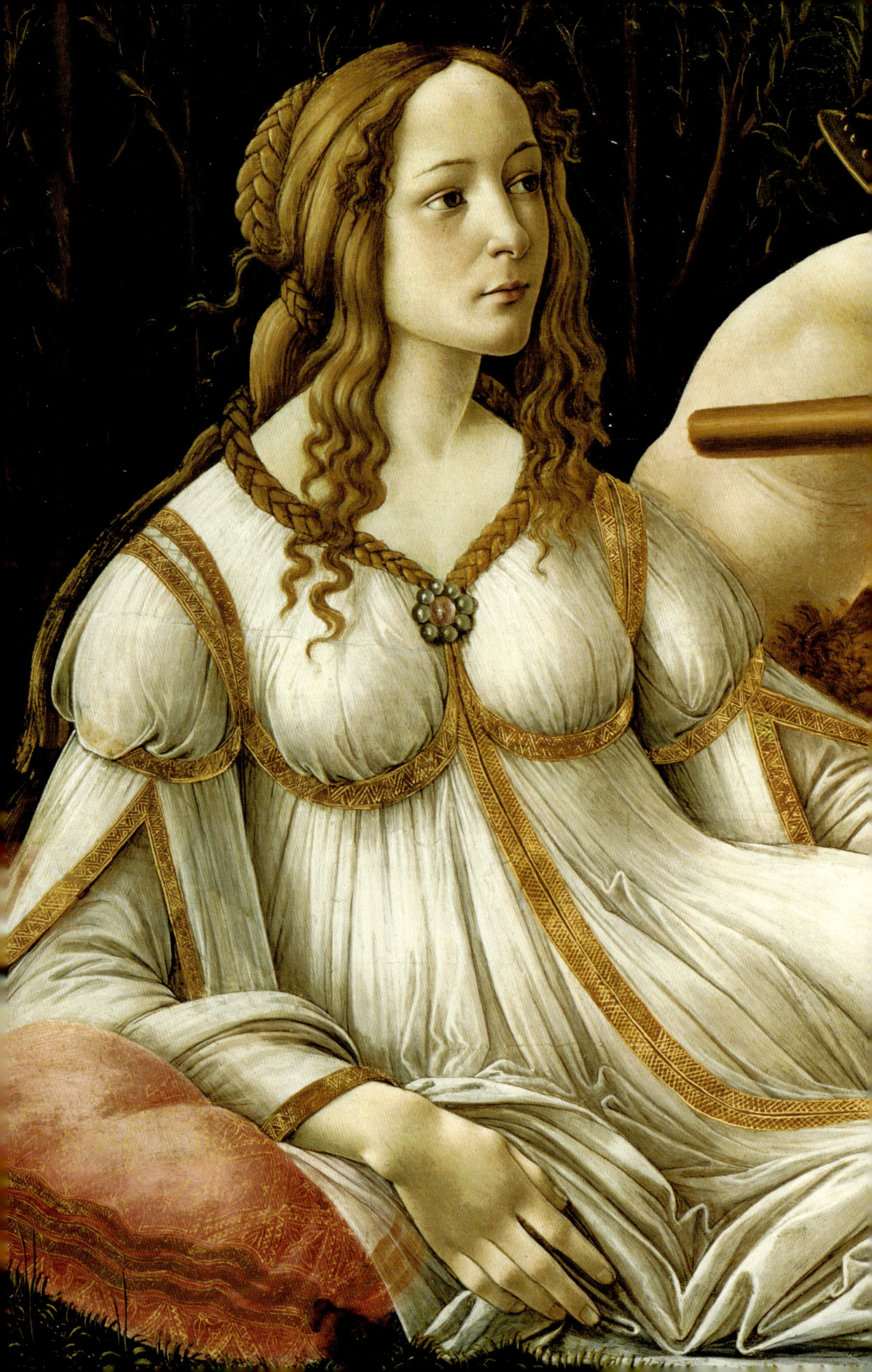

from other poets, or rather, stories related by the Greek and Latin historians, and likewise hunts, jousts, tales of love, and similar subjects, according to each man's particular pleasure.... And what is more, it was not only the chests that were painted in such a manner, but also the couches [*lettucci*], the wall-panels [*spalliere*], the mouldings [*cornici*] that went right round, and other similar magnificent ornaments for apartments which were used in those times, whereof an infinite number may be seen throughout the whole city. And for many years this fashion was so much in use that even the most excellent painters exercised themselves in such labours, without being ashamed, as many would be today, to paint and gild such things. And that this is true has been seen up to our own day from some chests, wall-panels, and mouldings, besides many other things, in the apartments of the Magnificent Lorenzo de' Medici, the Elder, whereon there were painted — by the hand, not of common painters, but of excellent masters... — all the jousts, tournaments, hunts, festivals, and other spectacles that took place in his times."[10]

In fact the majority of Botticelli's mythological paintings come into the category of decorations for chests, wall-panels, and bedsteads as described by Vasari — including *La Primavera, Minerva and the Centaur* and, most probably, *Mars and Venus.* In the latter, the foreground and middle ground are entirely occupied by two large and four smaller figures, with the tree-trunks and undergrowth of a small wood visible on the left. In the middle ground are some bushy twigs and to the right there is a hollow tree-trunk. In the centre of the picture the view opens out to show a green meadow, a range of mountains shimmering in the distance, and a section of clear blue, cloudless sky. The foreground is filled with

Venus clothed

two semi-reclining figures, a young woman dressed in white on the left, and a young man asleep on the right. He is almost nude, covered only by a skillfully draped white cloth. This combination of nude and clothed figures is itself striking and unusual, since in the fifteenth and sixteenth centuries most compositions had the female figure nude and the male figure clothed. While this may have some particular moral purpose, it may equally refer to the few classical depictions of Mars and Venus that were known at the time, because in these Mars was depicted nude whereas Venus was more or less clothed.

Four other, smaller figures also inhabit the rectangular picture space. They are indifferent to questions on clothing or nudity, for they are satyrs: mythological, faunlike creatures familiar from classical sources as Bacchus's wanton and often drunken companions.[11] Naturally these satyrs need no clothing, for their lower bodies are not human, but furry and hooved. Their heads are equally reminiscent of the animal kingdom, with small, curved horns peeping out from under endearing curls, and long pointed ears. These mischievous little fellows are playing with some obviously dangerous and warlike objects. The satyr to the left, depicted between the forest and the young woman in the foreground, has put on a helmet which quite clearly does not fit him, and in fact blocks his vision entirely. This gleaming head-protection, which is several sizes too large for him, also prevents him from seeing what the other satyrs are up to, which nevertheless does not stop him from precociously playing with a lance together with another satyr. Another satyr to the right is blowing into a large shell which he is holding up to the ear of the nude young man. The fourth satyr, in the

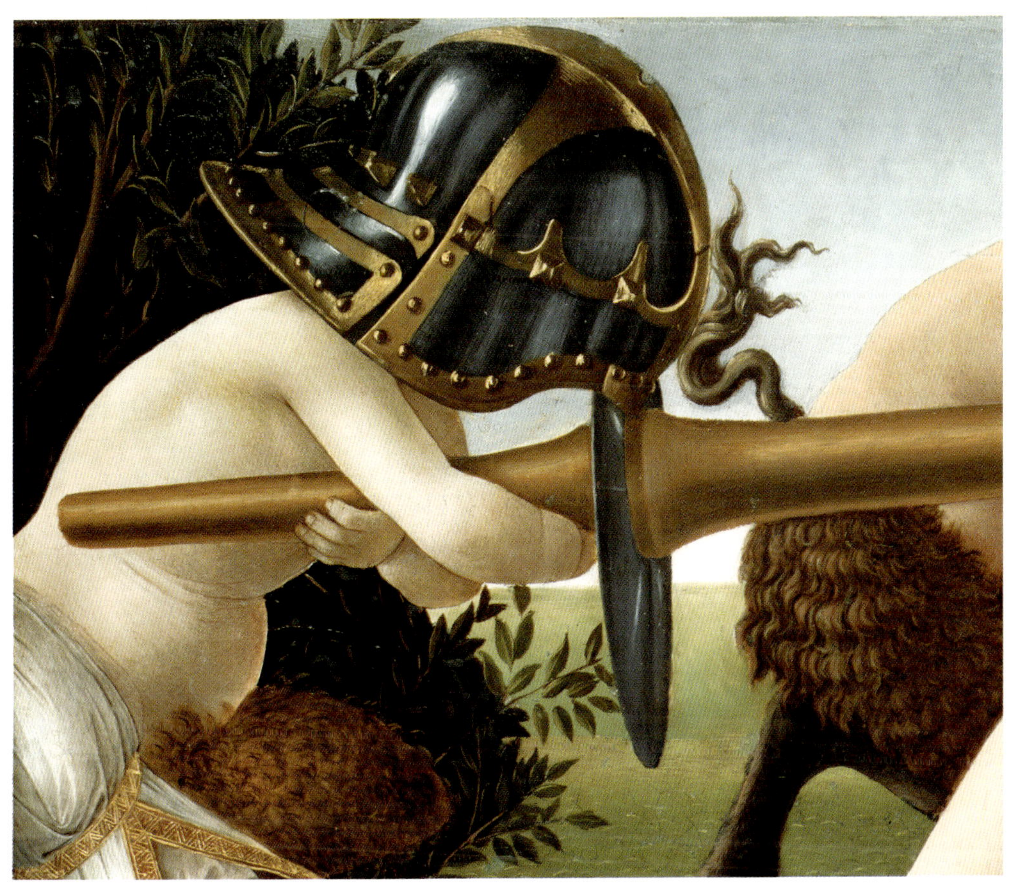

Satyr playing with a lance

Following two pages:
Sleeping Mars with satyrs

bottom right corner of the picture, has put on some armor and is reaching out his right hand towards the handle of a sword, on whose blade the young man seems to be lying despite any danger or discomfort this would surely cause. Here the accoutrements of war — helmet, armor, lance and sword — seen out of their usual combative context, clearly show that the recumbent male figure in this painting by Botticelli is Mars, the god of war. On the other hand, the clothed female figure opposite is not identifiable as Venus by virtue of her attributes, but — as we shall see — from the overall composition of the painting.

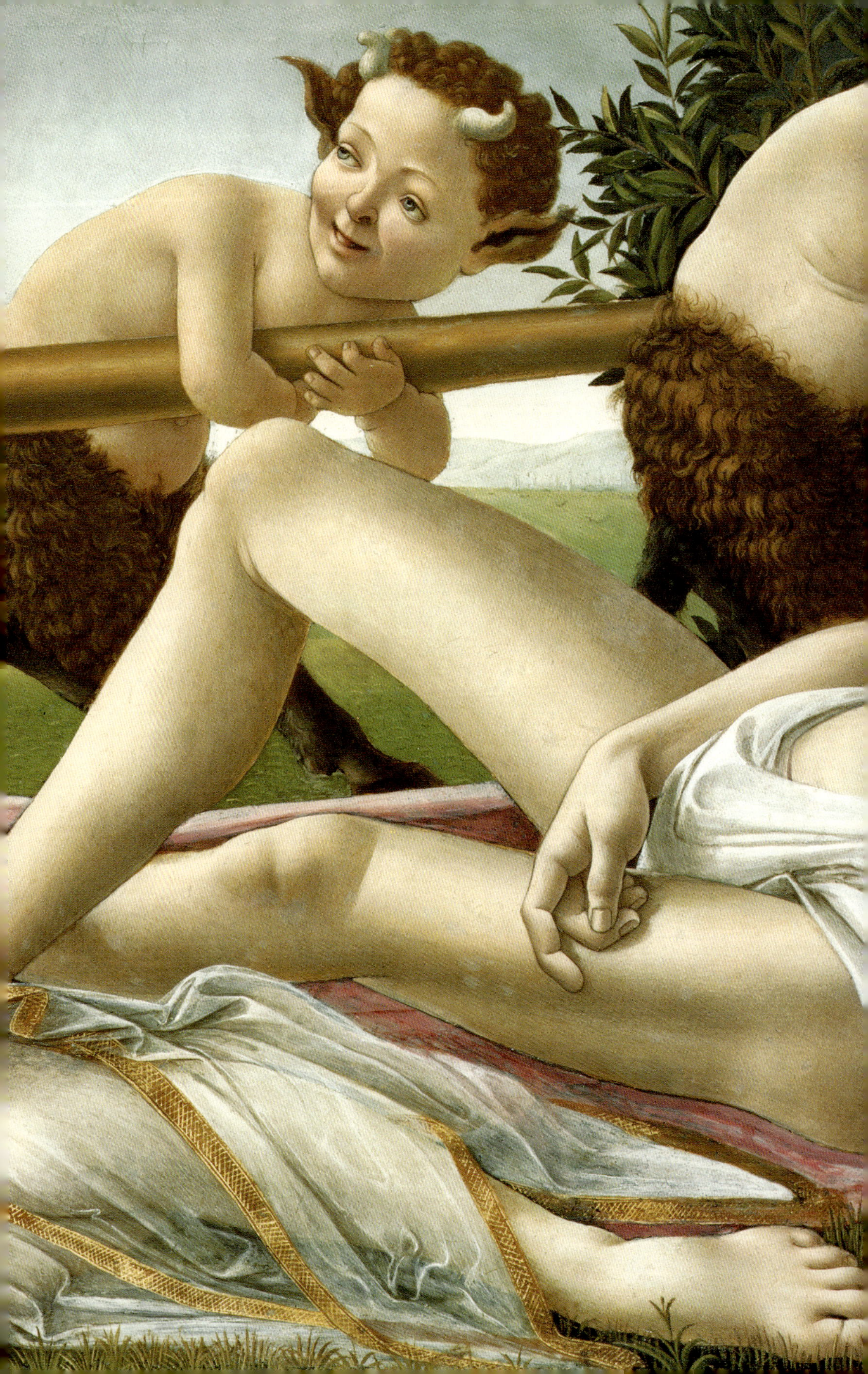

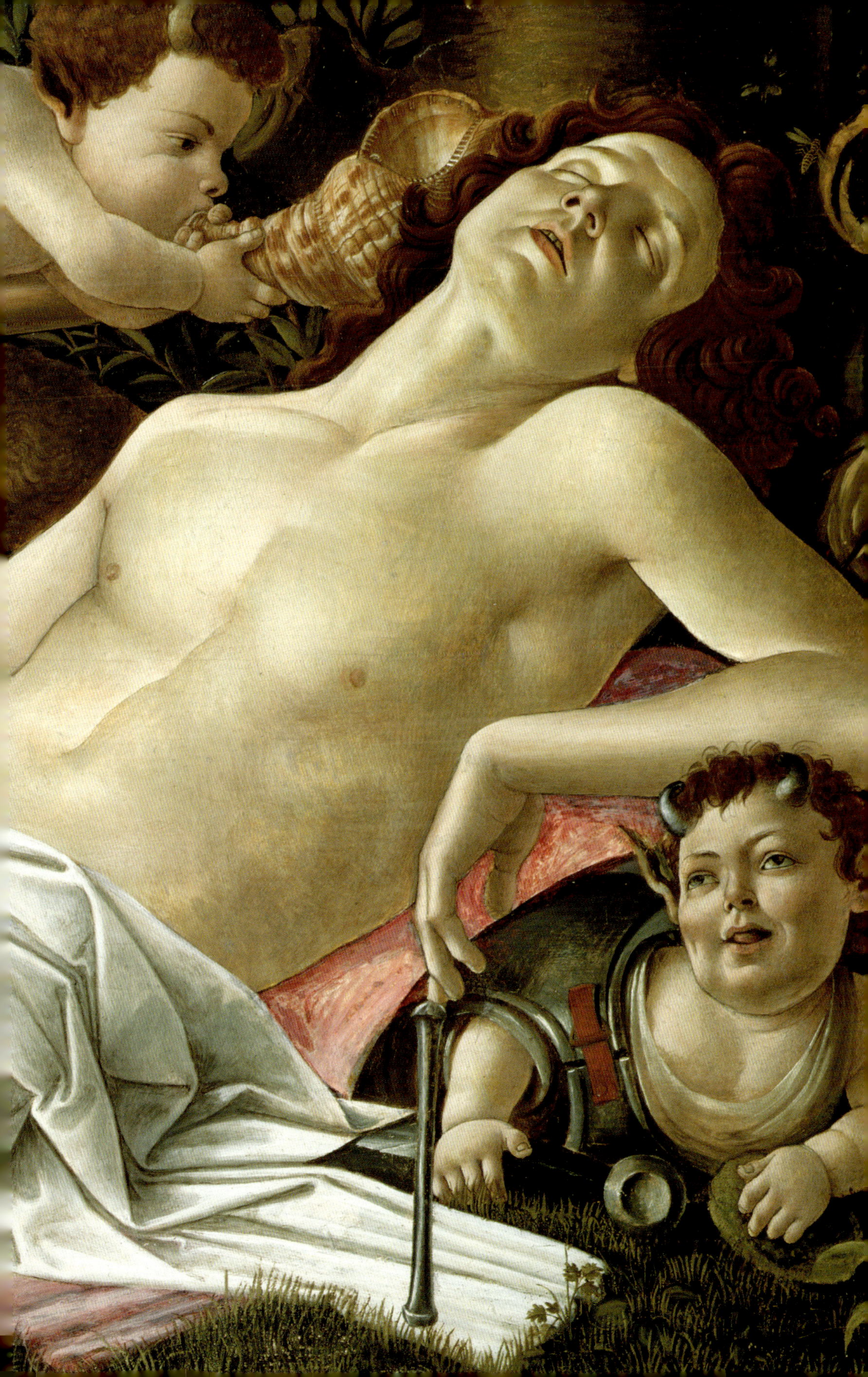

While large-scale paintings of classical gods and heroes first came into being during the age of Botticelli, in Western literature Mars and Venus were already commonly found together. Indeed, this "classic" pairing of the god of war and the goddess of love is found throughout the literature of antiquity, the Middle Ages, and the modern era, and Botticelli's painting draws heavily on these literary accounts. We read there not only of the god of war's bravery but also of his anger, his unpredictability, and his rancor which are apparently the inevitable side-effects of his warlike nature. And this is where Venus comes in, for it is her role to dispel or at least moderate the god of war's negative traits.[12] In 1469, a prominent contemporary of Botticelli's, the philosopher Marsilio Ficino, described the relationship of Mars and Venus in similar terms in his book *De amore.* In the chapter on the virtues of Eros he also describes the characteristics of Mars, the god of war, and the influence of Venus on those characteristics: "Mars is outstanding in strength among the planets because he makes men stronger, but Venus masters him.... Venus, when in conjunction with Mars, in opposition to him, or in reception ... often checks his malignance ... she seems to master and appease Mars, but Mars never masters Venus."[13]

The subduing of Mars by Venus and by love, as Ficino describes it here, is of course a well-known topos from the literature of classical antiquity. Lucretius, for example, in his *De rerum natura,* a philosophical didactic poem, vividly describes the characteristics of Mars as well as the necessary pacifying influence of the goddess of love on her warlike peer: "For thou alone canst delight mortals with quiet peace, since Mars mighty in battle rules the savage works of war, who often casts himself upon thy lap wholly vanquished by the ever-living wound of love, and thus looking upward with shapely neck thrown back feeds his eager eyes with love, gaping upon thee, goddess, and as he lies back his breath hangs upon thy lips."[14]

This description of the god of war, weary and resting, does at first remind us of the recumbent figure on the right in Botticelli's painting, for here too the exhausted Mars inclines his head gently backwards. Yet Botticelli's composition does not correspond exactly to this literary model because Mars is in no way gazing yearningly at the goddess of love. On the contrary, it would seem that, despite her breathtaking beauty, the young god has simply dropped off to sleep. Thus Botticelli did not merely illustrate a literary text; he varied an already quite visual description of the well-known theme of the enduring triumph of Venus over Mars, the topos of the taming of warlike, manly aggression by the pacifying force of womanly love. In order to explain the finer details of Botticelli's painting, however, we must refer to another source: an *ekphrasis* written by Lucian, that is, a classical picture description of the kind made famous above all by Philostratus. In Lucian's *Herodotos* we find a description of a picture by the classical painter Aetion. This painting, which was already lost in Botticelli's day, did not show Mars and Venus, but Alexander the Great and Roxana, the only woman Alexander ever really loved, who was later to become his wife. Lucian describes a composition which had distinct similarities with Botticelli's *Mars and Venus*: "On the other side of the picture, more Loves play among Alexander's armor; two are carrying his spear, as porters do a heavy beam; two more grasp the handles of the shield, tugging it along with another reclining on it, playing, I suppose; and then another has got into the breast plate, which lies hollow part upwards."[15]

Although this passage from classical literature does not correspond exactly to Botticelli's work (because the

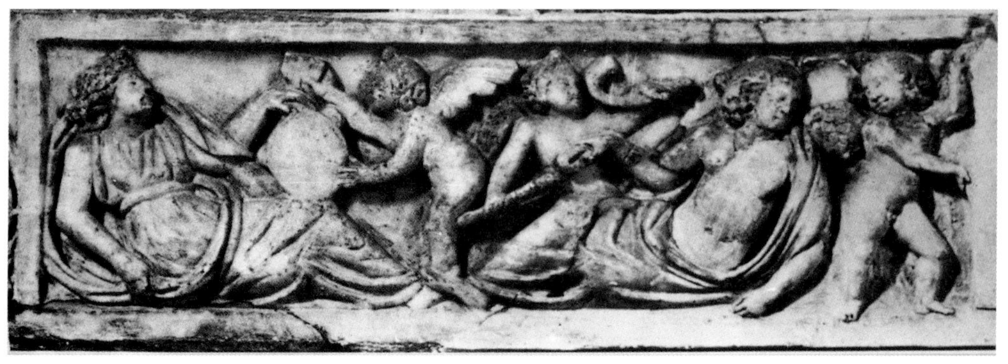

Detail of sarcophagus with Bacchus and Ariadne

subjects are Alexander and Roxana rather than Mars and Venus), the description of the little gods of love — the satyrs — has too many similarities with Botticelli's painting to be ignored: in Botticelli's picture they have a lance (equivalent to the "spear"); one of the satyrs has slipped into the armor — just as Lucian describes it; they are playing with the instruments of war. We can thus assume that two different types of sources had a direct influence on Botticelli's painting: a classical description of an image (the *ekphrasis*) and a contemporary account of an identical scene of Mars and Venus together.

In addition, there may have been a third source of inspiration for Botticelli's *Mars and Venus*. It is generally accepted that the formal model for Botticelli's composition was based on a relief sculpture showing the story of Bacchus and Ariadne on a classical sarcophagus in Rome, where it has remained to this day. Here too we find a semi-recumbent female figure opposite a reclining, apparently sleeping, male figure — although, as in Lucian's *ekphrasis,* this is again a classical source with a different theme, because on the sarcophagus relief the subjects are Ariadne and Bacchus rather than Venus and Mars. This difference was clearly not of concern to Botticelli and his patrons, for the formal world of the ancients was in itself interesting enough to provide models — particularly since profane iconography in the fifteenth century only had a relatively modest visual repertoire. Images borrowed from antiquity, whatever their subject matter, were consequently a welcomed aid to artists when it came to portraying mythological themes. It seems highly likely that Botticelli may have seen the sarcophagus in Rome, or at least a drawing of its decorative relief, but did not take too much account of its subject matter. He used the classical composition purely as a formal model to serve a quite different theme, albeit also from antiquity. There is one last, although perhaps less probable, connection in the context of the likely history of this painting. The legend depicted on the sarcophagus tells the story of Bacchus and Ariadne: she was abandoned by her lover Theseus on the island of Nexos, where Bacchus finds and comforts her, and eventually takes her as his wife. Thus the Roman sarcophagus refers to the mythological story of the nuptials of Bacchus and Ariadne. Since Botticelli's painting — as we shall see — was most probably painted for a wedding, it is not out of the question that the artist quite consciously drew upon a classical formal model which had marriage as its theme.

It is of course possible to interpret Botticelli's *Mars and Venus* in broadly philosophical terms if one takes this juxtaposition of god and goddess as an expression of the harmony of two opposites.[16] However, it may well be that a fact-based interpretation could be more useful and enlightening. Lucian can give us an indication of this possibility; the classical author precisely interprets his own picture description (the *ekphrasis*), which was an important source for Botticelli's painting: "All this is not idle fancy, on which the painter has been lavishing needless pains; he is hinting that Alexander has also another love, in War; though he loves Roxana, he does not forget his armor. And, by the way, there was some extra nuptial virtue in the picture itself ... for it did Aetion's wooing for him. He departed with a wedding of his own as a sort of pendant to that of Alexander; his groom's-man was the King; and the price of his marriage piece was a marriage."[17]

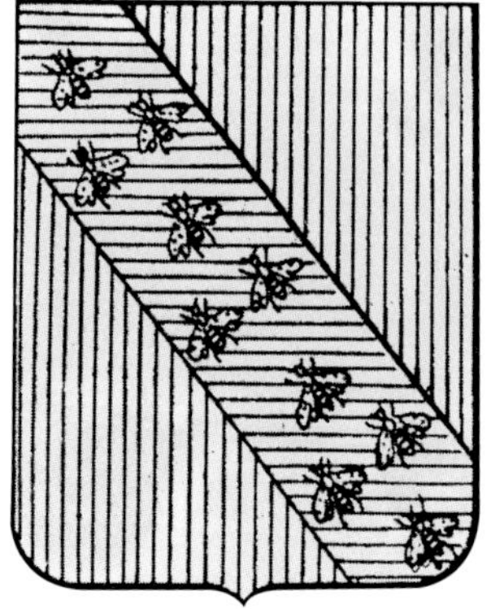

Vespucci family coat of arms

Thus the painting by Aetion which Lucian was describing was in itself a wedding picture, and the painter was rewarded by Alexander and Roxana with a wedding of his own. Since this literary source explicitly refers to a marriage, the next step for art historians is to look at Botticelli's patrons to see whose marriage might have been celebrated with a wedding piece showing Mars and Venus. And this line of enquiry is also the most reasonable because it takes into account concrete circumstances known to us from other works of art. On closer examination of the work itself a significant clue soon emerges in the shape of a small but important detail: on the far right there is a nest with wasps swarming out of it. This nest and the wasps themselves may be

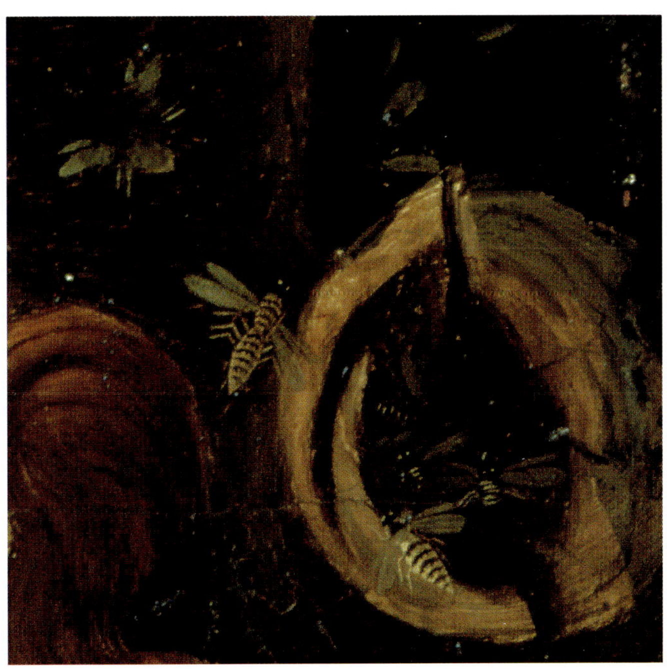

Wasps' nest

taken as an allusion to the Vespucci family. Vespa is Italian for "wasp," and for this reason the Vespucci family did indeed have a number of these insects on their coat of arms (see p. 26). The Vespucci (for example, Amerigo Vespucci who gave his name to the American continents) were a prominent, wealthy family with close political connections to the Medici. So far it has not been possible to link this painting with a specific wedding in this vast family, but the horizontal format of the painting, which is so reminiscent of paintings on wedding chests, has long made it seem likely that this painting was created for a wedding. And this likelihood is further supported by the inclusion of a myrtle twig in the background, since the myrtle was not only one of the attributes of Venus but was also a symbol of marriage.

Yet none of this explains the remarkable pose of the figure of Mars. The god of war could hardly be portrayed taking less interest in the scene around him, indeed he seems to have fallen asleep. His accoutrements of war — helmet, lance, armor and sword — have been turned into playthings by the satyrs. His sword no longer presents any danger to possible opponents. His body and facial expression appear equally relaxed and peaceful. The rosy flesh of his largely nude body does not look as though it has suffered harsh winds and weather, or been toughened by the hardships of battle. On the contrary, his skin seems rather to be delicate and soft, and its appearance by no means gives the impression of battle-hardened manliness. Stripped of his weapons, he needs only to be awakened in order to take up his duties as a lover. And it seems that this may be the purpose of the satyrs, one of whom is blowing into a shell to rudely awaken the god from his slumbers. For according to classical accounts, this wind instrument produces a particularly terrifying sound.[18]

On the one hand, Botticelli's painting of the slumbering Mars could be understood as a gallant compliment to the future bride who has subdued her stormy groom, as in the later portrayal of *Minerva and the Centaur*. But beyond this gallant compliment, the triumph of the goddess of love over the god of war also points to the gender-specific division of the roles of husband and wife as found in most patriarchal societies including that of fifteenth-century Florence. The utterly peaceful-looking form of the warlike god here represents the goddess of love's subjugation of the animal desire traditionally associated with the male, and in this specific case it probably also represents the domestication, as it were, of the possibly young groom whose passions are now to be safely contained within the bounds of marriage. The theme of the domestication of young men through marriage is a central theme of profane imagery, particularly in the last years of the quattrocento. The accepted view was that it was only in marriage that otherwise unfettered manly desires could find proper fulfilment, that is to say in the procreation of future generations.[19] And the task of controlling male freedom — originally associated with the unruly god Mars — can only be accomplished by chaste love, here embodied in a comparatively demure-looking Venus, who lies across from her spouse in a rather high-necked, white gown. Here the goddess of love, clad in pure white, represents the prospect of sensual pleasure, but only within the limits of marital fidelity. This apparent paradox of sensuality, which is virtuous by dint of being enjoyed within marriage, is perhaps also hinted at in the brooch on Venus's gown, namely in its symbolic design. White pearls signifying purity surround one red gemstone which probably symbolizes love and which is, metaphorically, held within bounds.

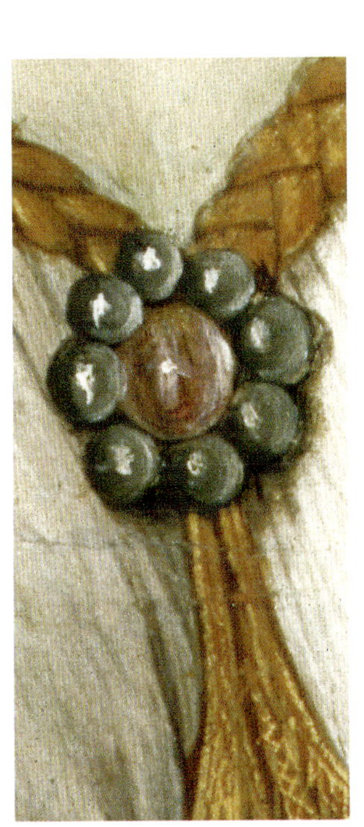

Brooch on the gown of Venus

One of the most interesting and at the same time complex aspects of classical mythology is its ambiguity. This of course applies to any picture of Mars and Venus. And indeed, here the theme of the subjugation of the god of war by the goddess of love, the domestication of fleshly desire by the chastely-dressed Venus, goes hand-in-hand with a tale of marital infidelity. For in certain classical accounts the husband of Venus is not Mars but the god Vulcan, who in fact one day discovers his wife in the arms of her lover. The theme of sensual love outside the confines of marriage is admittedly wholly absent from Botticelli's painting, and yet in its latent presence as an element in the classical Venus legend, it does indirectly bring to mind thoughts of sexual desire per se despite the clearly moral intention of the

Botticelli painting. Venus, the goddess of love, is not portrayed nude, and Mars, the incarnation of desire, is shown gently slumbering — yet the satyrs, as the embodiment of sensuality, are distinctly active: one is waking Mars up, another is smiling invitingly at the goddess of love, a third is wantonly showing his tongue between his half-opened lips. The subjugation of uncontrolled desires may be the main message of the picture — and the most important — but it is only one aspect of the work, for Botticelli does not completely suppress the eroticism of the scene. After all, it is difficult to portray the subjugation of desire without, at the same time, portraying desire itself.

Not least due to the ambiguity of mythological images, there were those who criticized this kind of painting even during Botticelli's own lifetime. The most ardent critic was the preacher Girolamo Savonarola, who was active in Florence at the time and extremely critical of what he saw as corruption in the Church and the lack of morals of his contemporaries. When it came to the practice of decorating wedding chests with stories from classical mythology, he raised the following objection: "And the houses of our leading families — what shall I say to these? No merchant's daughter weds without putting her dowry for safe-keeping into a chest that is not decorated with heathen tales. So the newly-wedded Christian maiden learns sooner of the deceit of Mars and the wiles of Vulcan than of the lives of the saintly women in both Testaments."[20]

Savonarola in fact exerted such great influence on the people of Florence that during the carnival of 1497 they publicly burned symbols of worldly desire and vanity — including many pictures with profane themes, fortunately Botticelli's *Mars and Venus* and others of his mythological works were not among these. It may well be that the pleasure which the owners took in these secular works prevailed over their religious devotion. Nevertheless, it should also be said that in the 1490s, Botticelli — that painter of "heathen tales" — was to be greatly influenced by the sermons of Savonarola, and that towards the end of his career he scarcely painted any mythological pictures.

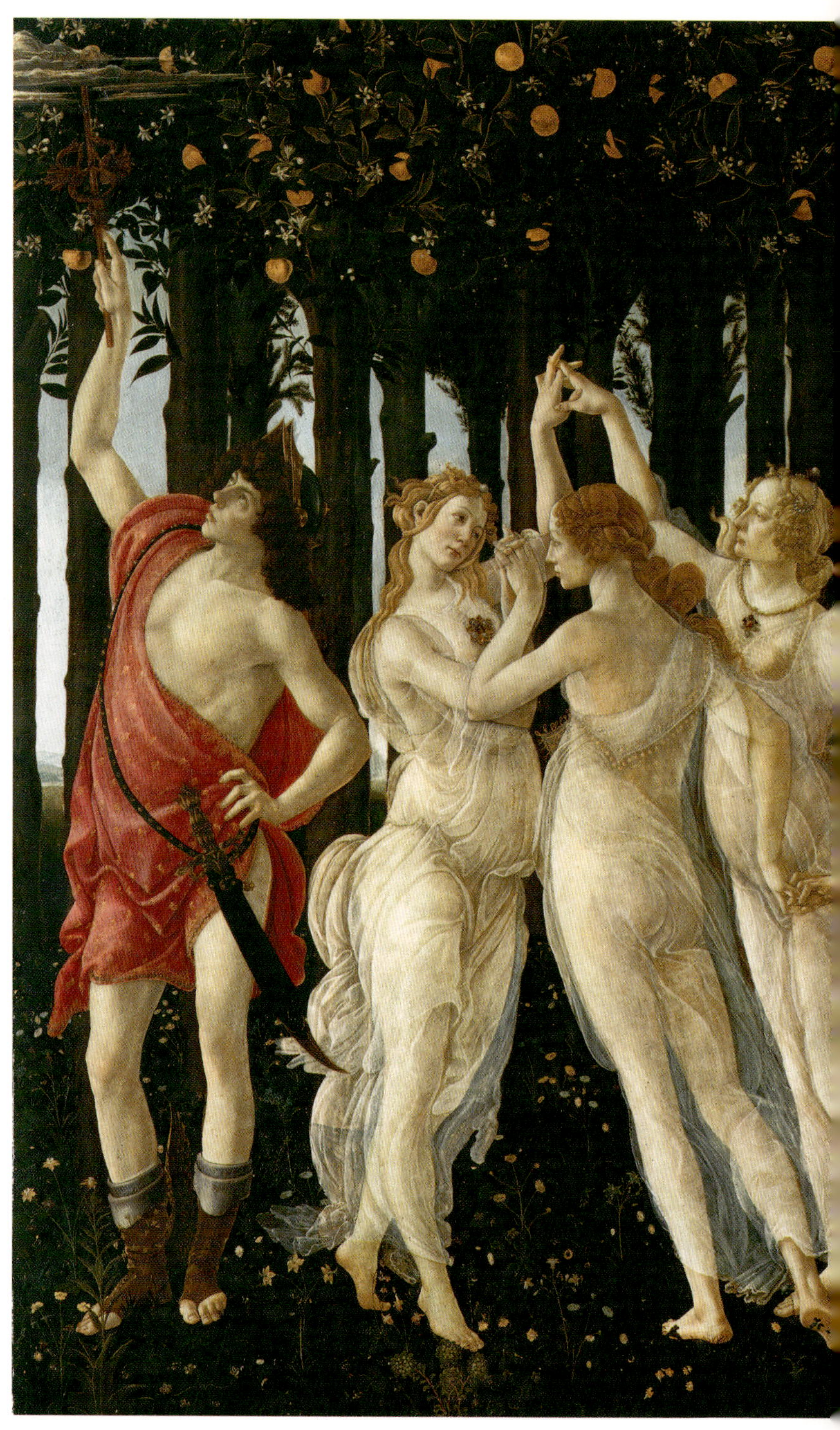

La Primavera, c. 1482

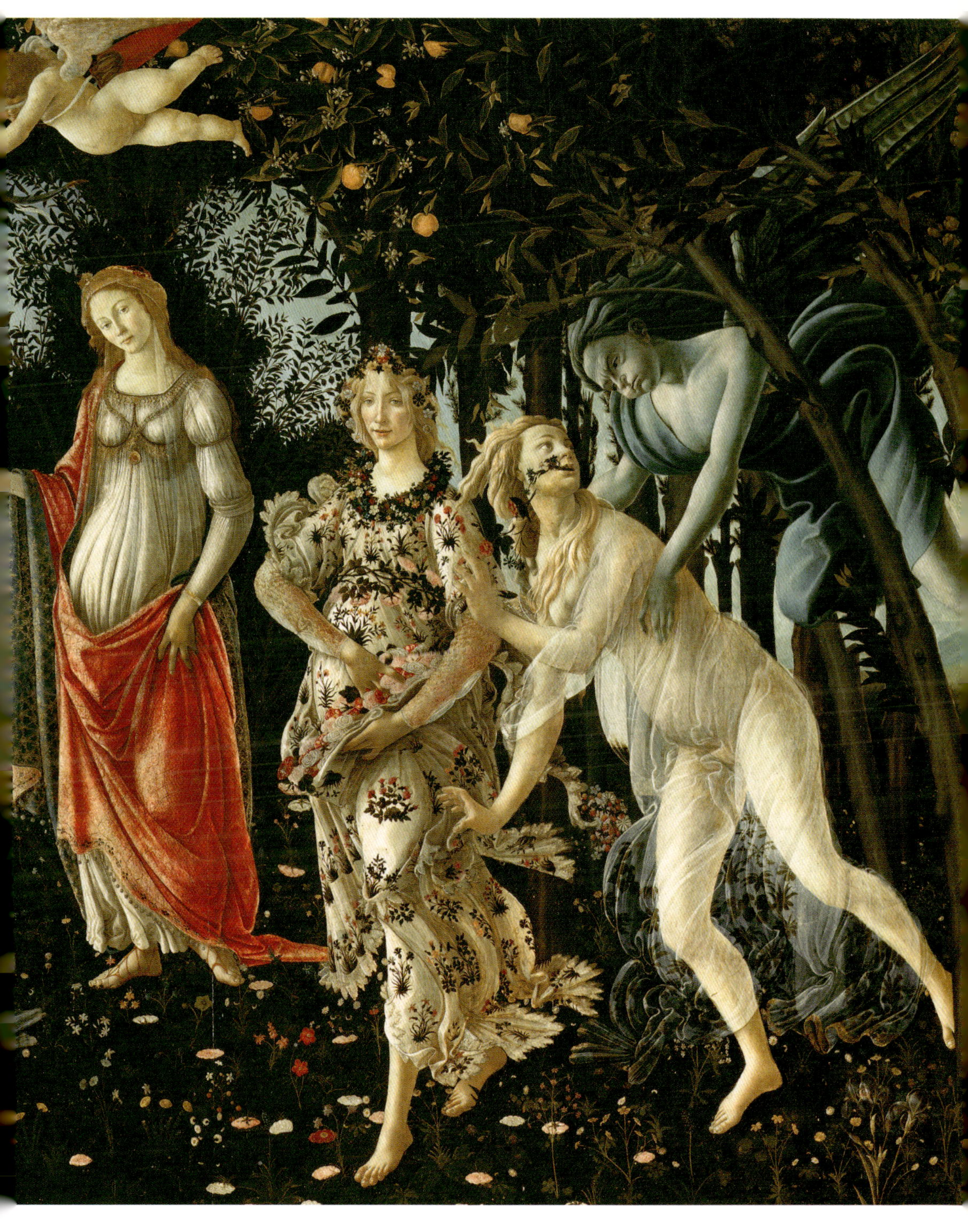

La Primavera: A Wedding Picture

Compared to *Mars and Venus,* Botticelli's *La Primavera* proves rather more difficult to interpret. The greater number of figures to be identified complicates the problem of interpretation; in addition to this there are numerous already existing interpretations, which ultimately confuse rather than clarify the issue. Giorgio Vasari takes a relatively easy way out in his interpretation of the picture; he describes Venus, decorated with flowers by the Graces, as an image of spring.[21] However, beyond pointing to the extraordinary charm of this work, he makes little further comment. He merely offers one piece of information which has influenced all subsequent interpretations, and ultimately only caused confusion. For Vasari mentions that both Botticelli's *La Primavera* and *The Birth of Venus* were located in a room of a country residence in Castello belonging to the Medici family. Until recently this has been taken to mean that these works were made together to decorate a country retreat belonging to Botticelli's patrons, that they were therefore thematically connected, and that particularly *La Primavera* — in this rural context — should be understood as a pictorial representation from the antique calendar describing the agricultural year.[22] However, close study of the household inventories of the Medici residences has radically altered the basis for any interpretation of *La Primavera*: this painting was in fact originally in the townhouse of the younger Medici family members in Florence, namely in the bedroom of Semiramide Appiani, who married Lorenzo di Pierfrancesco de' Medici

Mercury, the messenger of the gods

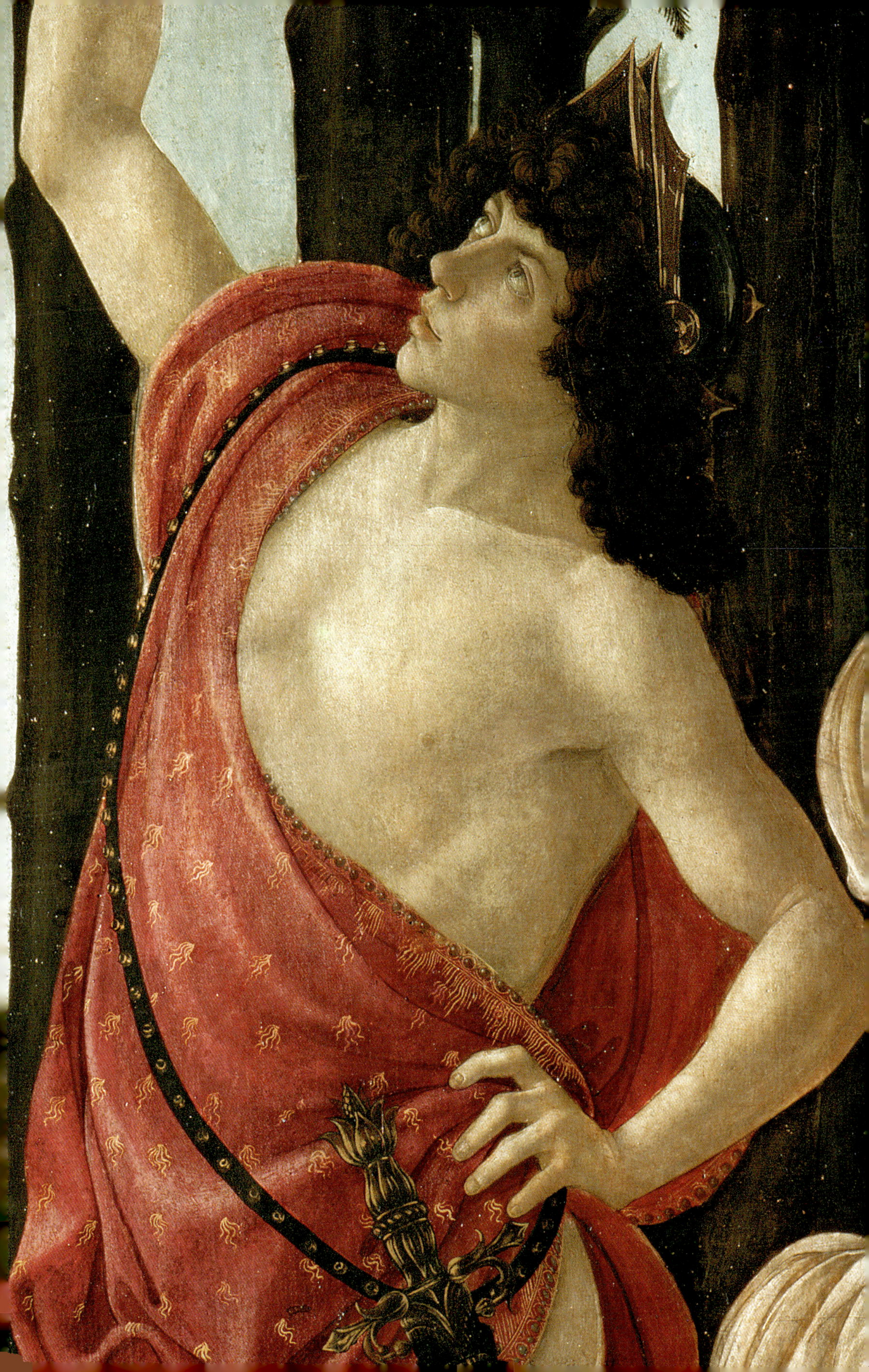

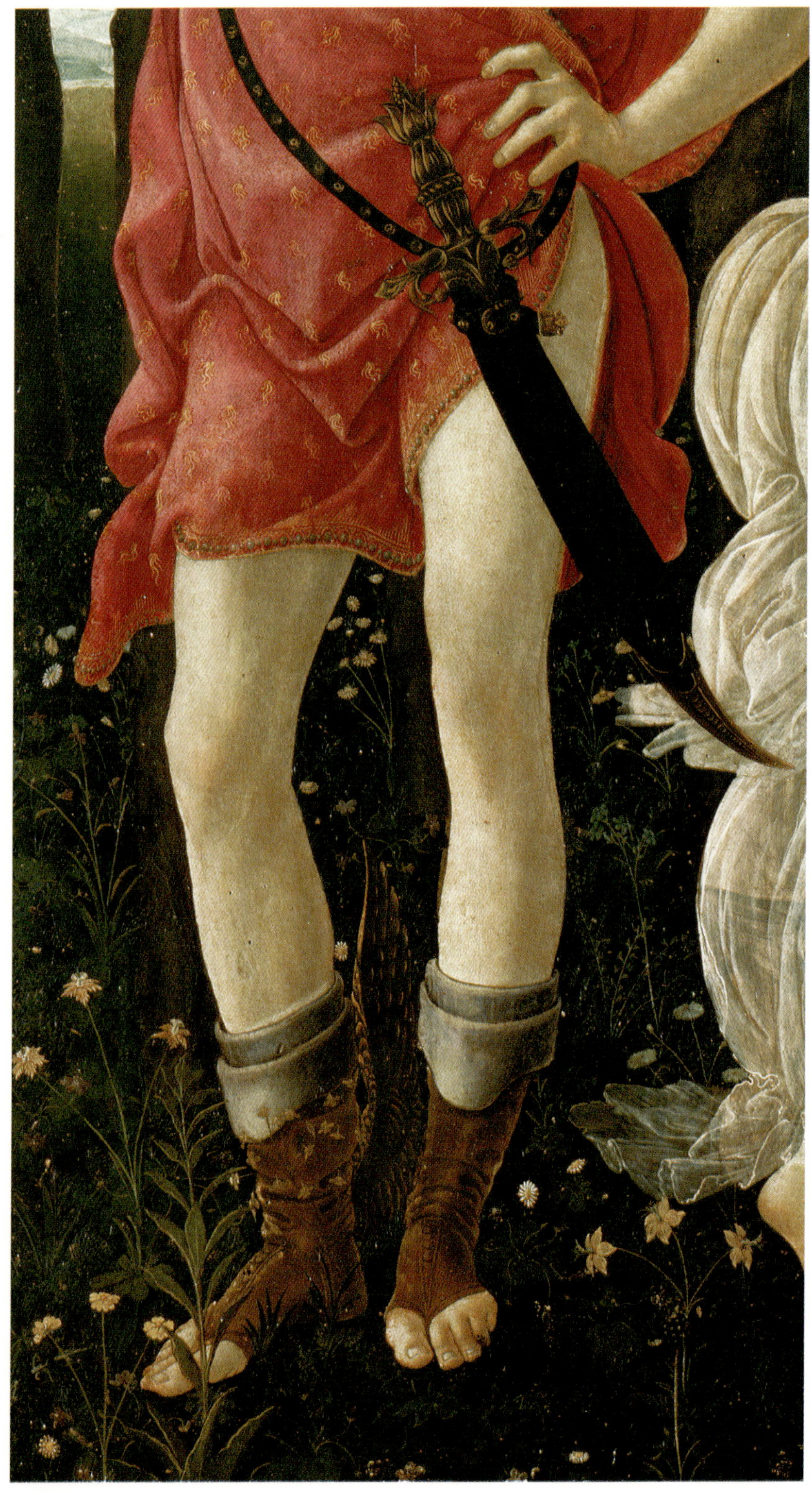

in the summer of 1482 after a good three years of negotiations. The mediator in this politically extremely important wedding was Lorenzo the Magnificent, the legal guardian of the groom, who was still a minor at the time, and Lorenzo is regarded as the family member who commissioned this work.[23] These circumstances must now be taken into account in any interpretation of this picture.

Painted in tempera on wood with a horizontal format and measuring nearly seven-by-ten feet (two-by-three metres), this work is accepted today as the largest fifteenth-century panel painting with a mythological theme. The work depicts a flower-filled meadow, a shady grove in the background with numerous slender trees, and nine figures including a putto floating above the others in the centre. On the left of the composition there is a young man wearing a red garment and a sword on a strap at his left hip. In his raised right hand he is holding a rod or wand. Next to him are three young ladies wearing transparent gowns and holding each others' hands. In the centre of the picture there is another, more modestly dressed, young woman who is lifting her right hand in a strange gesture. The putto above her is equipped with a bow and arrow, and he is blindfolded. To the right of the central figure there is another female figure who is stepping forwards and wearing a dress richly patterned with flowers. She is reaching into a pile of blossoms that fill a fold in her dress. Next to her is a young woman dressed in transparent white. She seems to be walking towards the woman next to her, but has her head turned to the figure on the far right of the composition, evidently a man with puffed-out cheeks who appears to be floating forwards out of the bushes and trees in the middle ground.

Winged shoes of Mercury

The viewer may well be able to identify various mythological personalities in the group of figures described here, but the overall meaning of the painting will remain a mystery if one is unfamiliar with certain underlying texts. No naive understanding is possible; no innocent eye would be able to contribute significantly to a full identification of the individuals portrayed here without having first read certain literary sources (see Literary Appendix on *La Primavera*). An informed viewer would soon notice that the young man at the left edge of the scene has wings on his shoes and that, with his snake-entwined rod, he is prodding a small bank of clouds or mist — evidently dividing or dispersing them. The snake-entwined rod (also known as a herald's wand or caduceus) and the winged shoes clearly identify this figure as Mercury, the son of Jupiter and the nymph Maia.[24] Mercury, the messenger of the gods as well as the god of merchants and thieves, was reputed to drive away the winter winds and was regarded as the harbinger of spring. More detailed information on his activities and on his snake-entwined rod may be found in Virgil's *Aeneid,* where he is described as a god dividing the winds and the clouds (*nubila*) with his wand (Appendix, no. 1). In interpreting the details in *La Primavera,* the last line a passage from the *Aeneid* is probably significant: "So shepherding the winds before him with his wand, he swam through the murk of the clouds." No other classical writer aside from Virgil in his *Aeneid* describes Mercury as dividing the wintry clouds. It is clear that in portraying Mercury with his wand in this manner, Botticelli is alluding specifically to the dispersing of the winter winds and the beginning of spring.

The flying cherub is just as identifiable as Mercury. The cherub is Amor, easily recognizable by his bow,

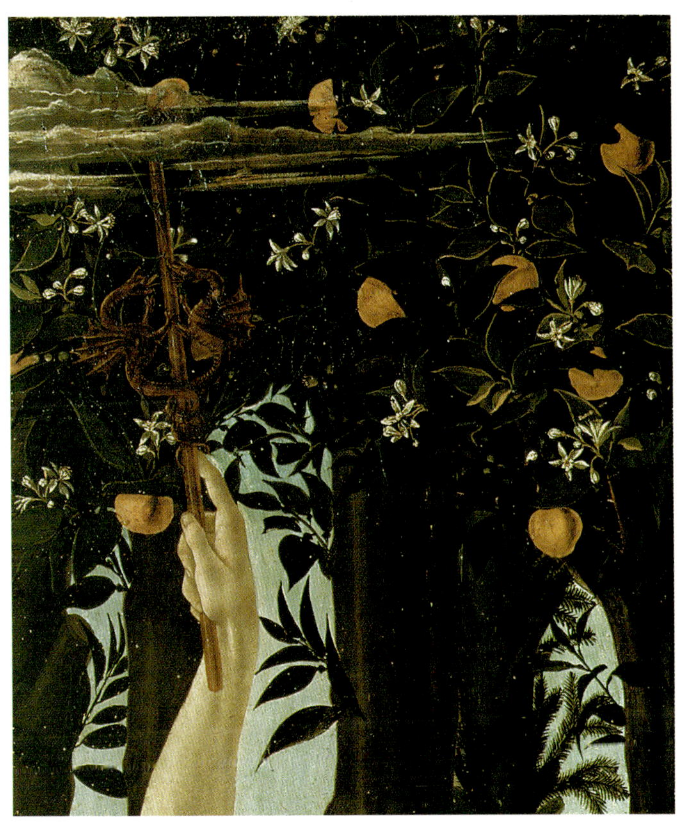

Snake-entwined rod of Mercury

arrows, and quiver as well as by his blindfold (see p. 41). Amor (known to the Greeks as Eros), the "winged son" of Mars and Venus, was the god of passionate love, described for example by Apuleius in the story of Amor and Psyche: "rash enough and hardy, who by his evil manners, condemning all public justice and law, armed with fire and arrows, running up and down in the nights from house to house, and corrupting the lawful marriages of every person, doth nothing (and yet he is not punished) but that which is evil."[25]

The young woman placed directly below Amor is his mother, Venus, the goddess of love and beauty. The group of young women dancing to her right are identifiable above all because they are three in number. These are the Three Graces, who frequently appear in the company of Venus and their guide Mercury. Their airy white gowns are further confirmation of their identity, for in both a classical source — Seneca's *De beneficiis* (*On Benefits*) — and in the art theory of the quattrocento — in Leon Battista Alberti's tract *On Painting* — the Graces are described as a group of lightly clad, dancing maidens who create an atmosphere of beauty and charm (Appendix, nos. 2–3).

Precisely the same configuration of Venus and Amor, the Three Graces, and Mercury is found in a well-known ode by the Roman poet Horace. In the second stanza, he not only describes the same figures but also refers to the Graces's loose clothing (Appendix, no. 4). However, compared to Mercury, the Three Graces, Venus, and Amor, it is much harder to identify the figures on the right side of the composition. Yet paintings are made to be understood, and therefore Botticelli decorated the young woman stepping forward, to the right of Venus, with countless symbolic flowers and blossoms. They cover her gown, adorn her hair and her neckline, encircle her high waistline, and fill a low fold low on the front of her dress. They correspond to the equally numerous flowers in the meadow where the scene is set, and make it more than likely that this young woman is Flora. This archaic Italian goddess of flowers and blossoms, of spring and of "good hope" for women is described together with Venus, Amor ("Venus's winged harbinger"), and another god, Zephyrus, by Lucretius in his philosophical didactic poem *De rerum natura* (Appendix, no. 5). Thus Botticelli was also drawing on this source which in fact links the right and left sides of the composition.

The goddess of spring, Flora, in fact owes her existence to a metamorphosis. Originally she was a nymph

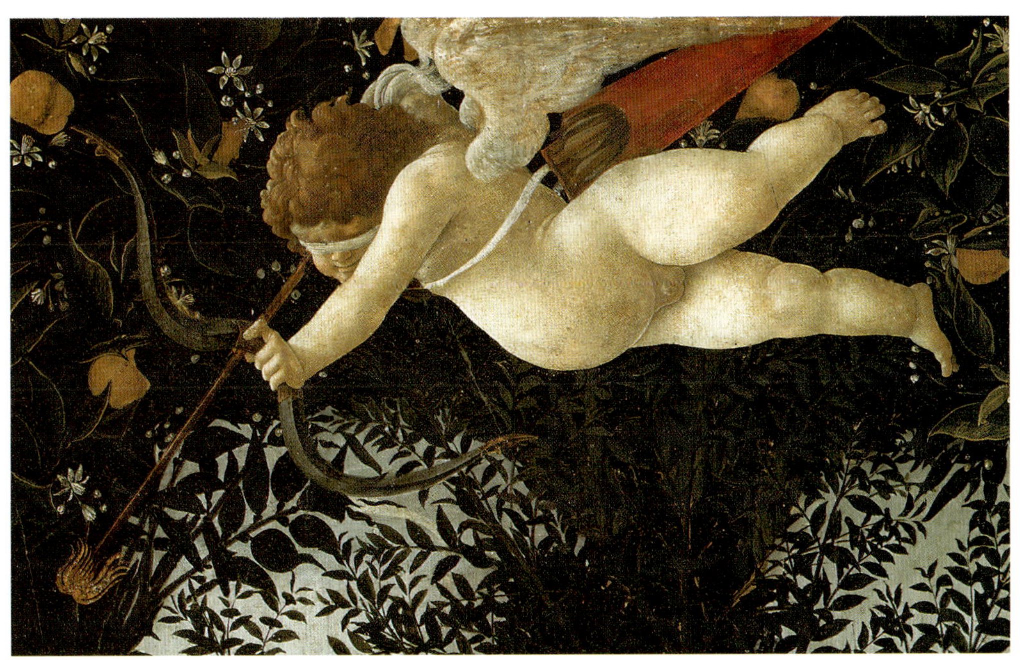

Amor, son of Venus

known by the Greek name of Chloris until she was touched by warming spring breezes in the shape of Zephyrus, the god of the west wind. This metamorphosis is described in Ovid's *Fasti,* a verse description of the months of the Roman calendar. One spring day the virginal nymph Chloris is wandering about in the open. When Zephyrus spots her, she flees; but he is far stronger and finally overpowers her (Appendix, no. 6). At the touch of Zephyrus she is transformed into Flora and breathes flowers out of her mouth, which is clearly portrayed by Botticelli in his painting, as well as her flight from Zephyrus and his touch. On the right side of Botticelli's composition, Zephyrus is further identifiable by his puffed-out cheeks and his wings, as well as the wind-blown trees bending before him. Even the numerous flowers in Botticelli's painting recall this particular passage in Ovid.

Yet more sources add to an even deeper understanding of this work.[26] Thus the burning arrow that Botticelli has given Amor may be an echo of Angelo Poliziano's *Stanze per la Giostra* (Verses for the Tournament), in which the eager cherub carries the same weapon.[27] The mood of this composition has also been compared with passages from Poliziano's *Rusticus,* Alberti's tract *On Painting* (Appendix, no. 3), and Seneca's *De beneficiis* (Appendix, no. 2), particularly concerning Botticelli's portrayal of the Three Graces dancing together in a circle and wearing gently flowing gowns, which in certain details also recall similar motifs in poetry of that period.[28] It is possible that Martianus Capella's *De nuptiis Philologiae et Mercurii* (On the wedding of Philology and Mercury), written around A.D. 400, may also have had an influence. There too the winged messenger is described as the harbinger of spring and the guarantor of fertility — a motif which Botticelli has depicted in the plant seeds floating gently downwards next to Mercury[29] (see p. 36). Taken together, these sources — Virgil, Lucretius, Horace and Ovid — fully reveal the identity of the figures in this painting and offer a suitable explanation of the contents of the picture.

One could say, therefore, that the composition of *La Primavera* and the figures it contains are largely inspired by a bold combination of various text fragments. Few other outstanding artworks are based on a comparably deliberate combination of literary sources. It even seems possible to order these texts according to their importance for the painting's message. Indeed the left side of the picture — up to Venus and Amor — may be seen as little more than an array of barely connected figures. The right side of the picture, however, is much more dynamic; two of the figures are in motion and, in one

Chloris and Zephyrus

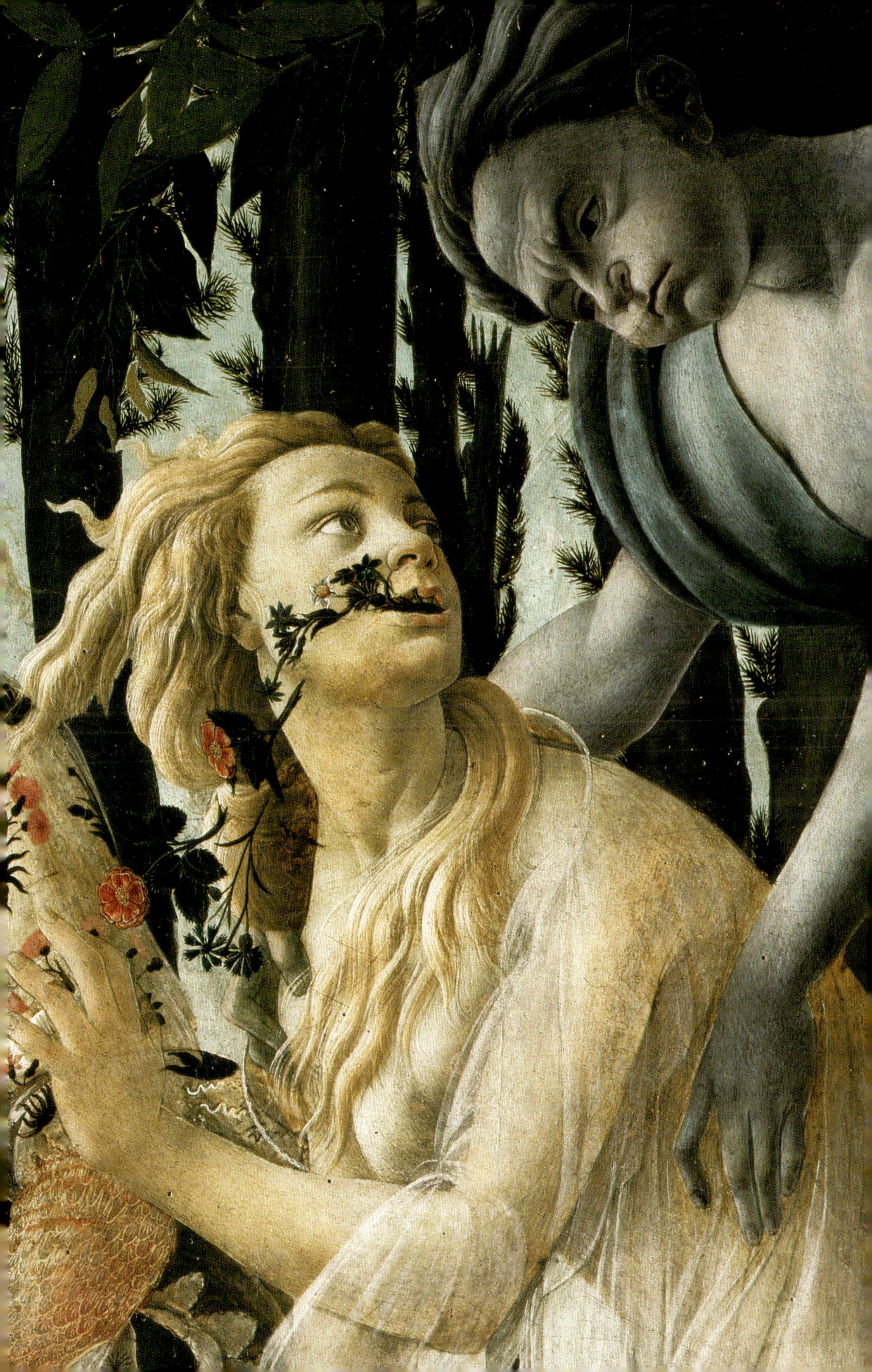

case, a figure is even in the process of changing her identity. The contrast between the comparatively static scene on the left and the more active scene on the right also reflects the literary sources, in that the passage in Ovid's *Fasti,* which relates to the right of the composition, is itself much more lively and dramatic than the relevant sections of Horace, Virgil and Lucretius.

The Ovid text is therefore the most significant source, for unlike the others it does not merely name the most important characters involved but also gives a description of the relevant action in the scene. The transformation of the nymph Chloris into Flora, described in the *Fasti* and dramatically portrayed by Botticelli, shows clearly that the picture is connected with the subject of marriage, for Zephyrus not only transforms the once virginal nymph into Flora, the goddess of spring, but at the same time takes her as his wife — according to Ovid. In addition to the marriage itself, in the relevant passage Ovid also speaks of the dowry, the property and money that the bride brought with her into the marriage, which in quattrocento Florence constituted the most important status symbol in any wedding. He also describes the blossoming garden as a metaphor for the fertility which the bride was expected to bring to the marriage. Later in the text Flora remarks that, although Zephyrus initially took her by force (*rapina*), he more than made amends for this by his loving behaviour as a husband. She has no cause for complaint in her marriage bed; it is now eternally spring for her. She has a wonderful garden in the lands which she brought with her dowry. Everything is green there all year long — trees and meadows alike — for her spouse has filled this garden with blossoming flowers and has made her, Flora, the mistress of this magnificent display of flowers and blossoms. Thus the most important literary text behind the picture makes repeated allusions to the subject of marriage, even to the fact that in those days the bride frequently had little or no say in the choice of husband, and therefore might well have felt the marriage to be an act of violence committed against her.[30]

It is not only the literary sources that *La Primavera* draws on which reveal it to be a wedding picture. This is also suggested by the information mentioned above regarding its original location in the old townhouse of the Medici family in the Via Larga in Florence. There, in a *camera* (room) next to Lorenzo di Pierfrancesco de' Medici's own, the painting was integrated into the headboard structure of a *lettuccio*. Thus, *La Primavera* was intended for the bride's chamber. Its symbolism is in keeping with that of the so-called "*lettuccio* pictures," while in broader terms the work also has much in common with paintings created in conjunction with the *spalliere* (see p. 15), which drew on the tradition of decorative frescoes in secular surroundings.[31] The actual occasion for the commission of this work was the wedding we have already mentioned between Lorenzo di Pierfrancesco de' Medici and Semiramide Appiani.

Following this same line of thought, it is also possible to identify a clear order of importance in the pictorial *dramatis personae* involved in this work; thus Zephyrus represents Lorenzo di Pierfrancesco de' Medici and Flora the bride, Semiramide Appiani, for in Ovid's *Fasti* these two are named as husband and wife. It must be said, however, that these figures are not clearly identifiable by virtue of the similarity of their features to their real-life equivalents. If anything, these are allegorical portraits which rely for their effect less on physiognomic recognizability than on the readily comprehensible ordering

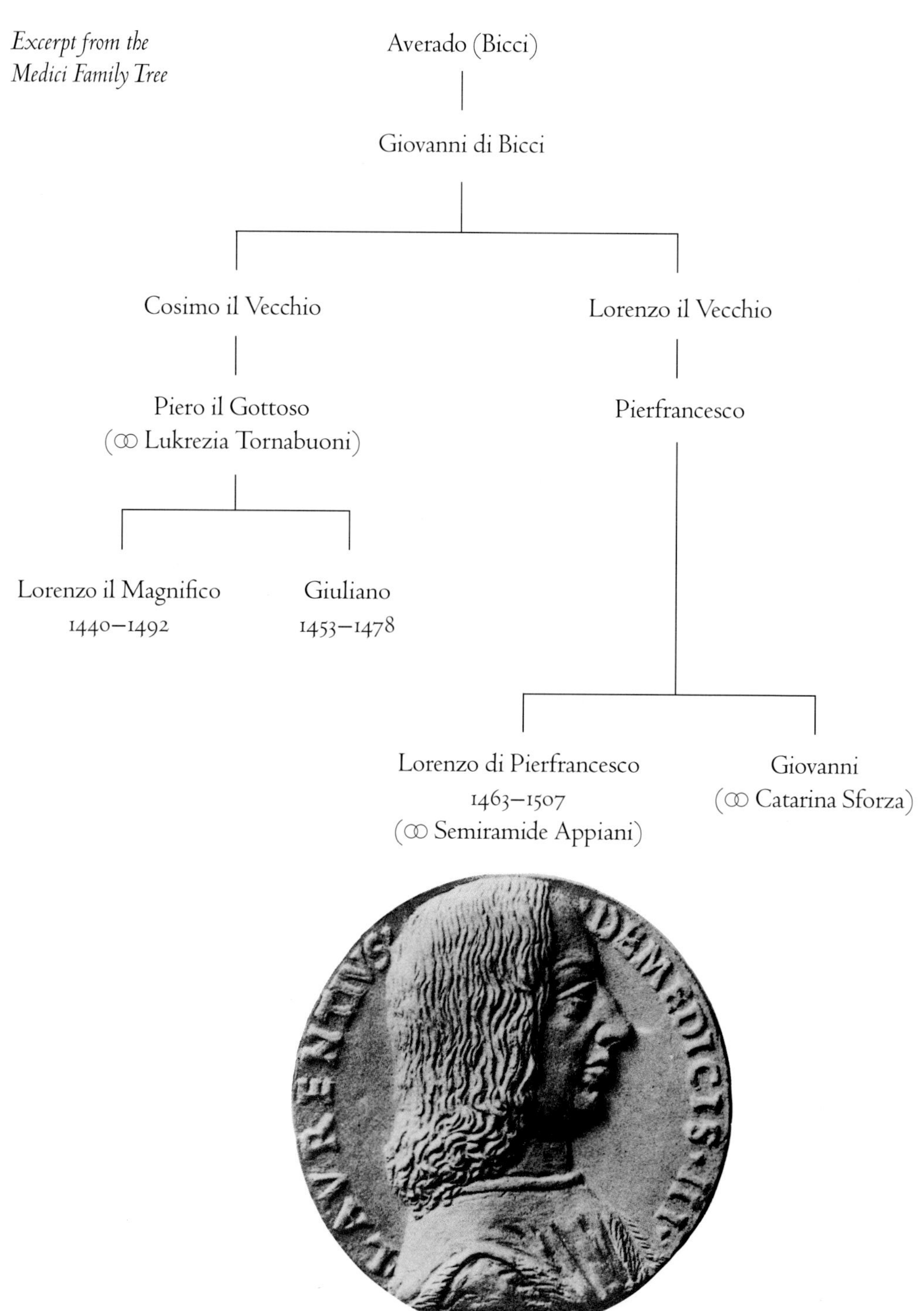

Italian, late 15th century
Portrait Medallion of Lorenzo di Pierfrancesco de' Medici

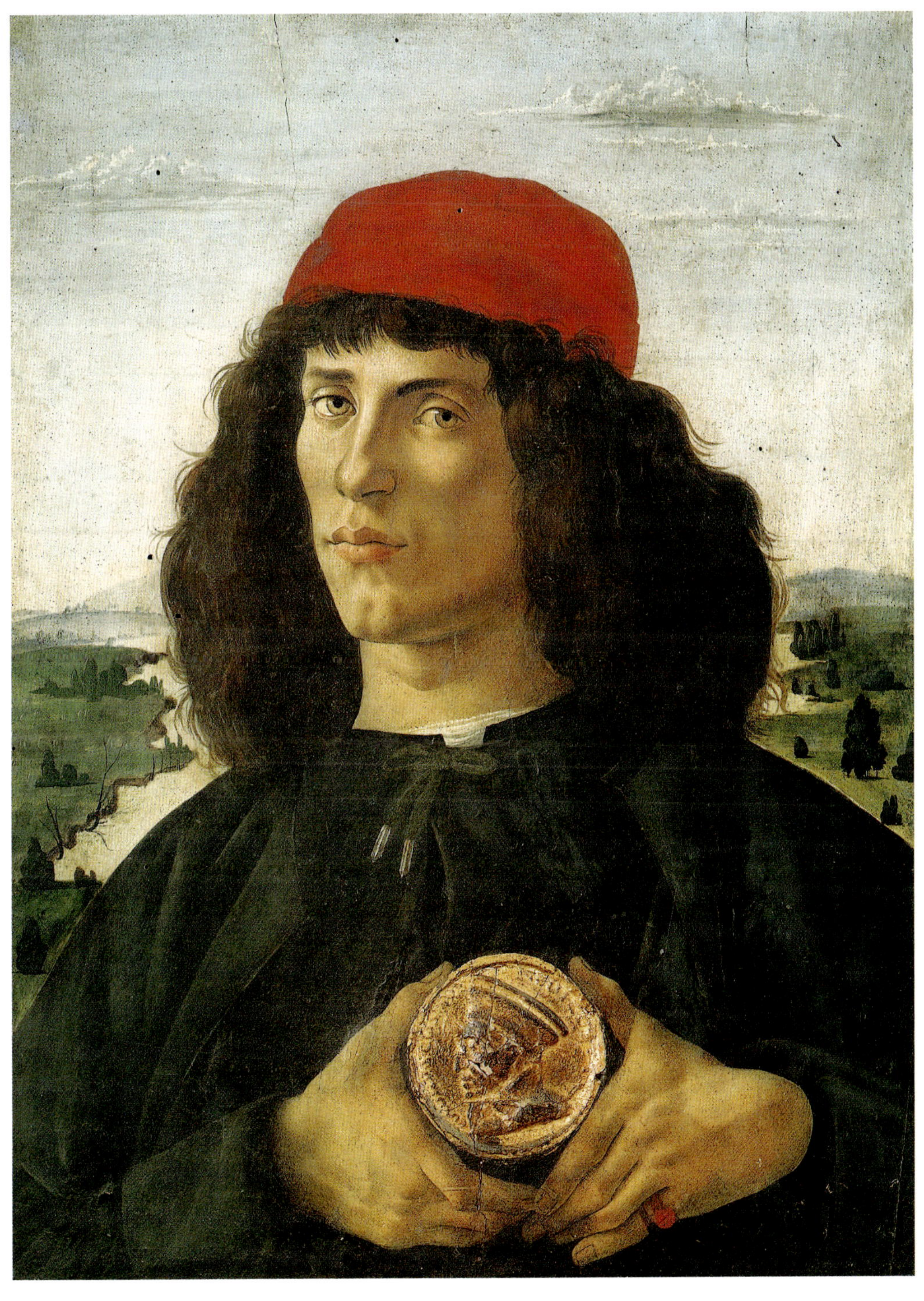

Sandro Botticelli
Portrait of a Man with a Medal of Cosimo the Elder, c. 1475

of the characters and their roles according to Ovid's text and the historical situation at the time of the wedding. In this sense, perhaps there is also a connection between Mercury and Lorenzo the Magnificent who had arranged the wedding. As the guide of the Graces and as the god who drives away the winter winds, Mercury could be identified with Lorenzo the Magnificent who had, metaphorically, created a propitious climate for the wedding, just as Mercury is doing when he drives away the winter winds in the painting. In fact, Mercury's features do display a certain similarity to those of the subject in Botticelli's *Portrait of a Man with a Medal of Cosimo the Elder* (see p. 47), which has recently been identified as a portrait of the youthful Lorenzo the Magnificent before he had been worn down by life and fate.[32] The strongest physiognomic similarities are in the irregular nose, the high cheekbones, and the already somewhat sunken cheeks and full lips.

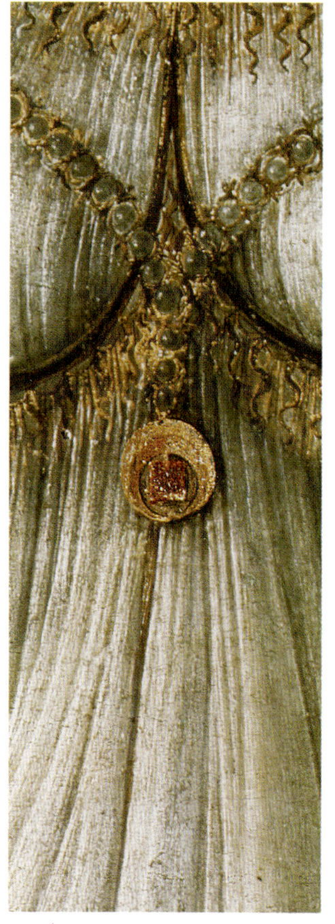

Crescent-moon amulet of Venus

The Iconography of Womanly Virtue and Marriage

Venus is not only the goddess of love and of beauty, but also the divine protectress of weddings and marriage,[33] so Botticelli surrounds her with myrtle twigs, traditionally associated with weddings and childbirth but also with sexual desire.[34] Thus the central figure in Botticelli's *La Primavera* expresses the notion of sexuality as it should ideally be found after the wedding and within the confines of marriage. There are additional nuances of this theme in other details. For example, the goddess of love in *La Primavera* — as before in Botticelli's *Mars and Venus* — is not nude but dressed. As a type, this too is a chaste Venus, who has less to do with extra-marital

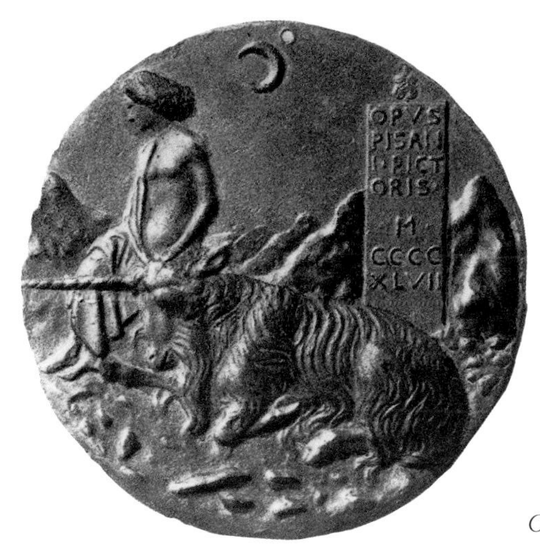

Antonio Pisanello
Portrait Medallion of Cecilia Gonzaga (verso)

desire and unfettered sensuality than with the idea of regulated and productive fertility within the context of marriage; this is in itself in keeping with the idea of a newly-founded family.[35] With this apparent paradox of chaste fertility, Botticelli's *La Primavera* presents a favorite theme in contemporary wedding pictures of that period. Similarly, the *spalliere* depicting the story of Nastagio degli Onesti made by Botticelli and his assistants illustrate, among many themes, the idea that it is only acceptable to "spend" oneself sexually within the constraints of marriage and for the procreation of future generations.[36]

A reinforcement of this idea of sexual desire tempered by marital chastity is hinted at in the goddess of love's amulet which depicts a crescent moon (see p. 48). The crescent moon was traditionally regarded as an attribute of the chaste Diana, the goddess of hunting who resisted all suitors, even covering her body in dirt and filth in order to repel her most ardent admirers. In keeping with this tradition, the crescent moon was understood in the visual arts as a symbol of chastity. There are several examples of this in fifteenth-century art. Notable among these is a portrait medallion of Cecilia Gonzaga by the artist Pisanello (see p. 49). On the reverse side of this medallion, the artist depicts a seated figure (presumably Cecilia again), whose chastity is underscored by the presence of a unicorn (which according to legend could only be caught by a virgin) and further emphasized by a crescent moon.[37] The crescent moon amulet worn by the fully-dressed Venus figure in Botticelli's *La Primavera* is clearly part of this iconographic tradition and, in that sense, stands for the ideal of chaste love.

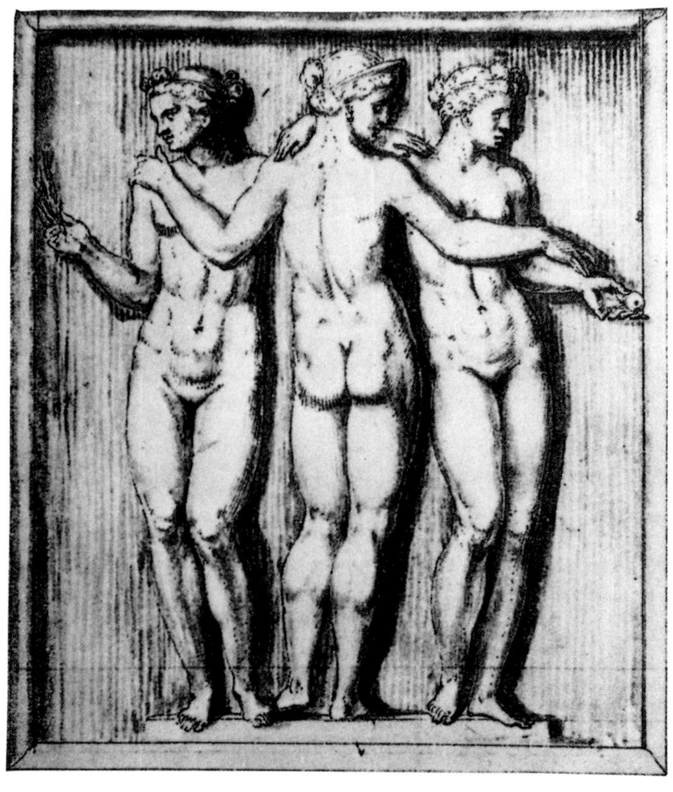

Drawing of the Three Graces in the *Codex Coburgensis,* c. 1550

Right page: Three Graces

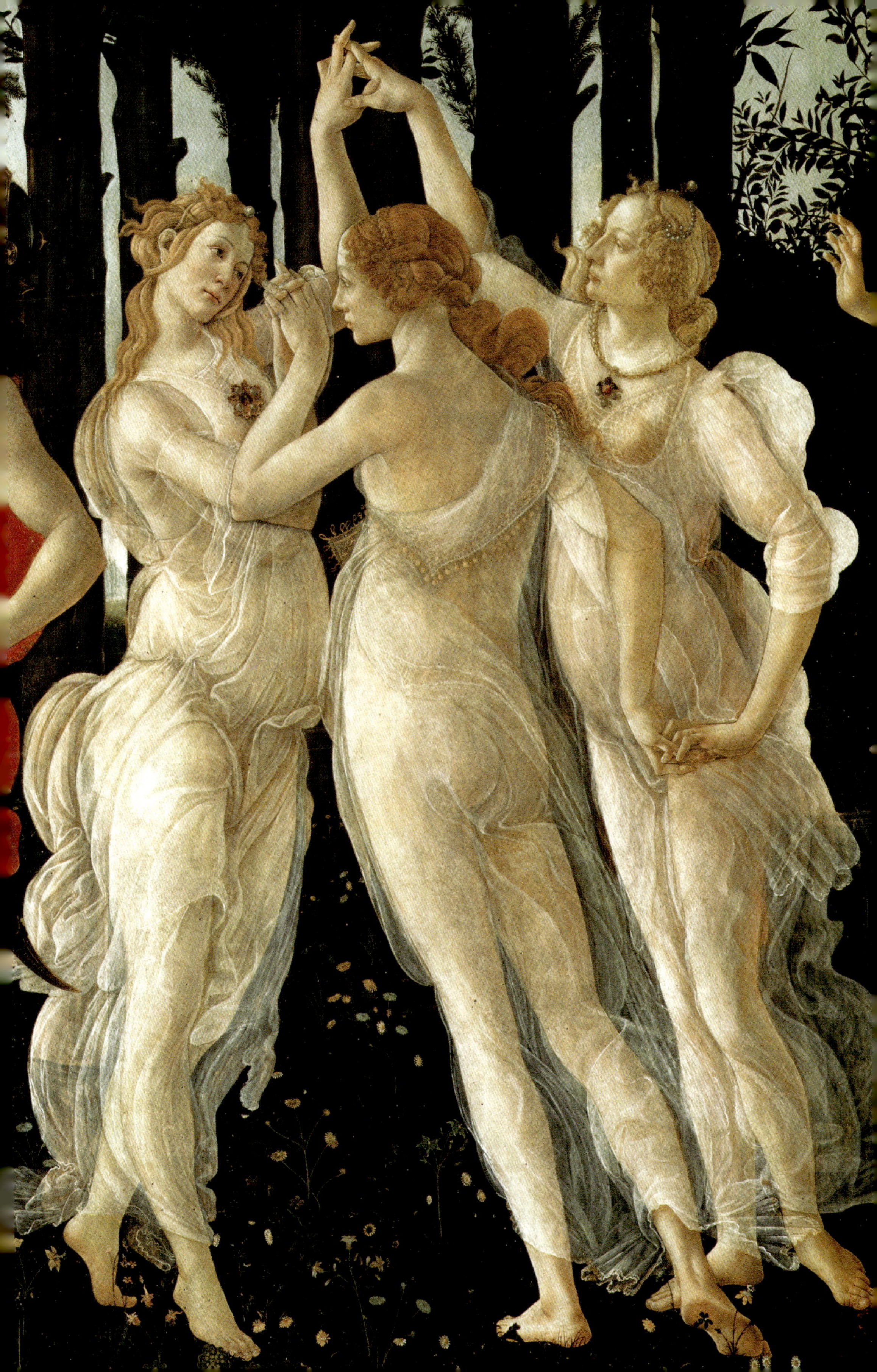

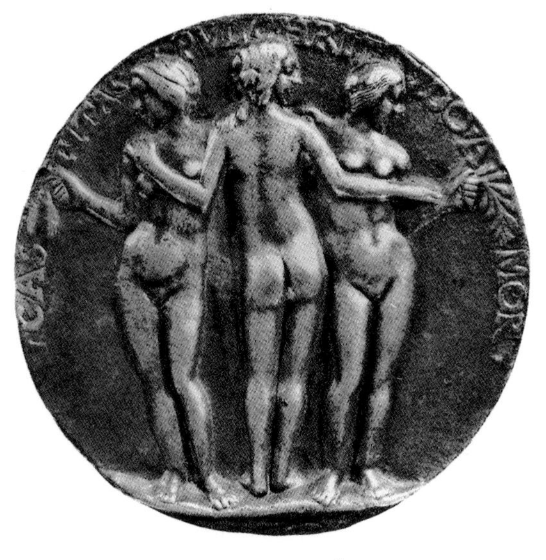

Attributed to Niccolò Fiorentino
Portrait Medallion of Giovanna Albizzi (verso), 1486

Symbols of marriage and womanly virtues, such as beauty and chastity which have already been identified in the complex figure of Venus, are even more evident in the remaining figures in the left half of the composition, namely in the combination of Mercury, Venus and the Three Graces. Forms employed for the portrayal of the Three Graces during the Renaissance often echoed motifs from classical sculpture that were already familiar to artists in the fourteenth century, and which Botticelli (in *La Primavera*) and other artists (see p. 50) varied freely. In general terms the Graces usually present a charming scene of young women dancing, whose cheerful mood is expressed, for example, in their loose, flowing clothing (Appendix, no. 2). Naturally, depending on the context, there were a number of interpretations of the Graces in the fifteenth and sixteenth centuries; portrayed in the context of particular circumstances, for example, they could serve as concrete evidence of the transfiguring power of womanly virtue. On the occasion of the marriage of Isabella d'Aragona and Gian Galeazzo Sforza in Milan, for example, the Three Graces were among the allegorical characters included in a truly magnificent wedding celebration. The festivities were organized and directed by two Florentine artists, none other than Leonardo da Vinci and the poet Bernardo Bellincioni, who had occasionally worked for Lorenzo the Magnificent up until 1482. The climax of their so-called *festa del paradiso* was the appearance of the Three Graces together with Mercury, seven nymphs, and personifications of the seven virtues at the close of a ball which lasted all night. The Graces sang a song of praise to the bride,

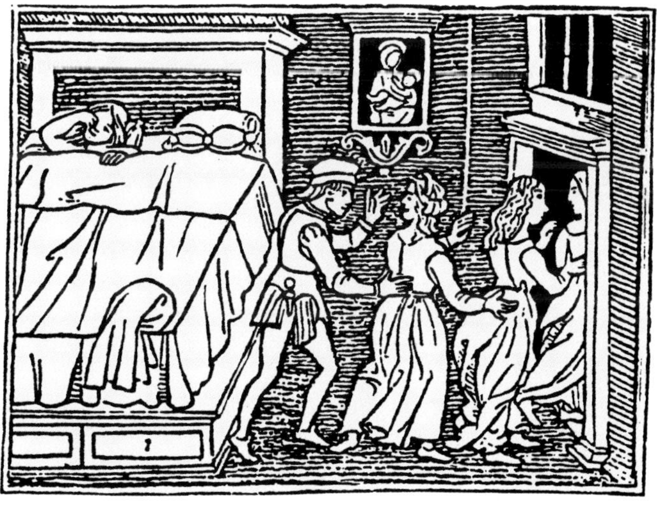

Woodcut illustration from *Questo sia la nobilissima historia de Maria per Ravenna,* c. 1480

telling the company that it was only her virtue that made their presence possible; without Isabella's virtuous character they would not have been able to attend the festivities. Following this, the Cardinal Virtues sang praises of the newly-married bride before entering the bridal chamber with Isabella and the Graces. This "transfiguration"

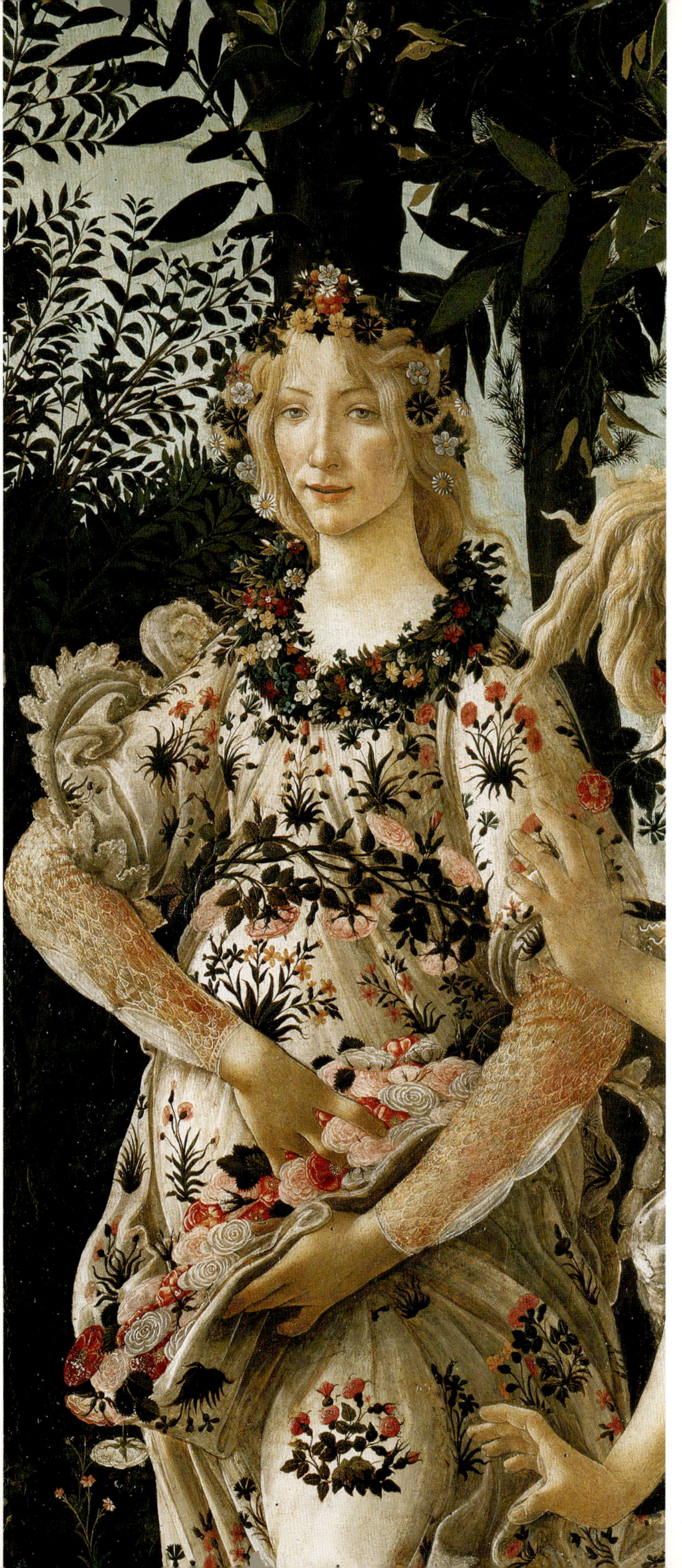

Flora,
the goddess
of spring

of the bride's virtues was the final climax of the festivities, and then, what happened behind closed doors, must be left to our imagination.[38] In any event, no doubt, the groom sooner or later sent the Graces on their way again — at least this would seem to be the case according to a fifteenth-century woodcut illustration showing a newly-married bridal couple (see p. 53). The bride, who is already undressed, is lying in bed and awaiting her fate while the young husband is persuading the three young ladies to leave the room.

The Three Graces, as an unmistakable allusion to womanly virtue, also appear on the reverse of a portrait medallion of Giovanna Albizzi (see p. 52). Made on the occasion of her marriage to Lorenzo Tornabuoni in 1486, the front of the medallion shows a profile portrait of the bride. On the reverse there is an inscription which identifies the Graces as Chastity, Beauty and Love — *castitas, pulchritudo* and *amor*. These allusions in the images of the Three Graces and the link between chastity, beauty, and love are a striking reflection of the demands that were generally made in those days (by men) of women and, in particular, of married women.[39] In this context, womanly beauty was not understood as a self-justifying quality that merely consisted of physical charms; on the contrary, it was seen as the direct consequence of virtue. This close connection between external beauty and important inner values is explained by Alberti in his tract *Della Famiglia* (The Family): "Among the most essential criteria of beauty in a woman is an honorable manner.... In a bride, therefore, a man must first seek beauty of mind, that is, good conduct and virtue."[40] A similar concept is conveyed by the inscription on a Florentine wedding chest: "There is no beauty without virtue, and without love there is no loveliness."[41] Physical beauty could not be separated from either spiritual beauty nor, consequently, from virtuous behaviour. This ideal of virtue is seen personified in the Three Graces in Botticelli's *La Primavera.*

Flora: Tree of Plenty for the Medici Family

The allusions to marriage in *La Primavera* and its literary sources of course go hand-in-hand with the bride's desire for fertility and children. Accordingly, the theme of fertility is not only expressed in the numerous blossoms and ripe oranges in the painting, but also in the figure of Flora, who is scattering white and red roses from a low fold in the front of her dress — a clear reference to the progeny to be expected from her womb. In addition to these general references to fertility, procreation, and progeny, there is yet another iconographic element which once again underlines this painting's function as a wedding picture. Flora's exact position in the painting is by no means a matter of chance, for — having just been transformed into the goddess of spring — she is stepping forward but has stopped at a particular moment. Her left leg is almost stationary and, together with her slender body, forms a vertical which runs from her left foot on the ground right up through the tree behind her. This direct vertical link — a kind of oneness — between the figure and the tree is unusual and certainly unique in Botticelli's work. Any thoughts of an accidental union of figure and tree may be readily dismissed, for the whole effect of *La Primavera* relies on the care with which the artist lavished on every last detail, including an orange tree (*citrus aurantium*) which bears both blossoms and fruit. In fifteenth-century Florence oranges were known as *mala medica* or *palle medicee*: symbols of the

Fruit-bearing orange tree

Medici family.[42] Their symbolism was based on fact. Since the fourteenth century, a small orange grove grew in the courtyard of the old Medici palace, and was regarded as a kind of barometer measuring the flow of the family's history. In the sixteenth century, Giulio de' Medici (the nephew of Lorenzo the Magnificent) referred to the fact that the condition of these trees and their fertility had always been an omen for the fate of his family. The inclusion of the orange tree in this painting was of great significance to the Medici family.[43]

The connection between the fruit-bearing tree and Flora with the fruit of the Medici, who had commissioned this work, is carefully constructed on the right side of the picture, reading from the outer edge towards the centre. Here again we see the meticulous subtlety of the artist's thinking. Zephyrus himself is positioned in the laurel tree, the *lauro nobilis,* a clear allusion to the groom, Lorenzo — in Latin *Laurentius* — whose name is visualized here. It is notable that, in the upper right corner of Botticelli's picture, there are neither blossoms nor oranges to be seen in the trees: indeed this area appears far from fruitful. It is only to the left of this, in the section where the touch of Zephyrus has transformed Chloris into Flora, that the situation changes — for the orange grove with its blossoms and fruits begins at precisely the point where there is a line running from Flora through the tree behind her. Thus the transformed figure of Flora marks the start of the "fruit-bearing" section of the composition. The goddess of spring may also be understood as the trunk of the fruit-bearing tree, whose fertility will come to fulfilment — as indicated in the blossoms and fruits — at Lorenzo's touch. Considering Ovid and the dynamics of the painting, Semiramide Appiani (as Flora) will therefore become the bearer of the Medici fruits and progeny only at Lorenzo's touch, following their union as man and wife. This depiction of the "function" of the bride and married woman would certainly have been readily understood by viewers of that time; especially those who would have had access to the bride's *camera*. Here, it was the procreation of future generations rather than sexual desire which was seen as the real purpose of sexual relations and marriage.[44]

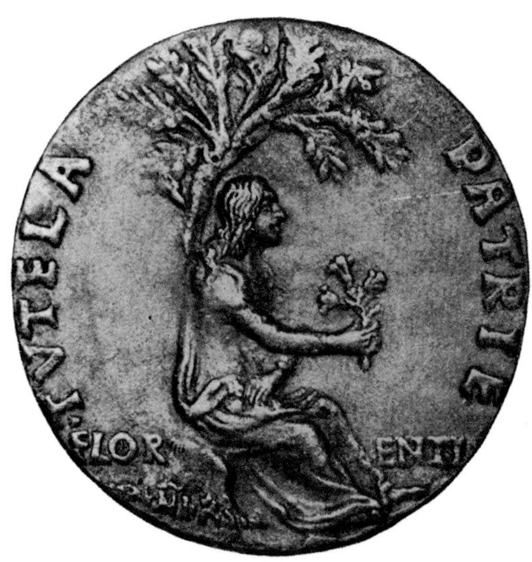

Attributed to
Niccolò Fiorentino
Portrait Medallion of Lorenzo il Magnifico
(verso)

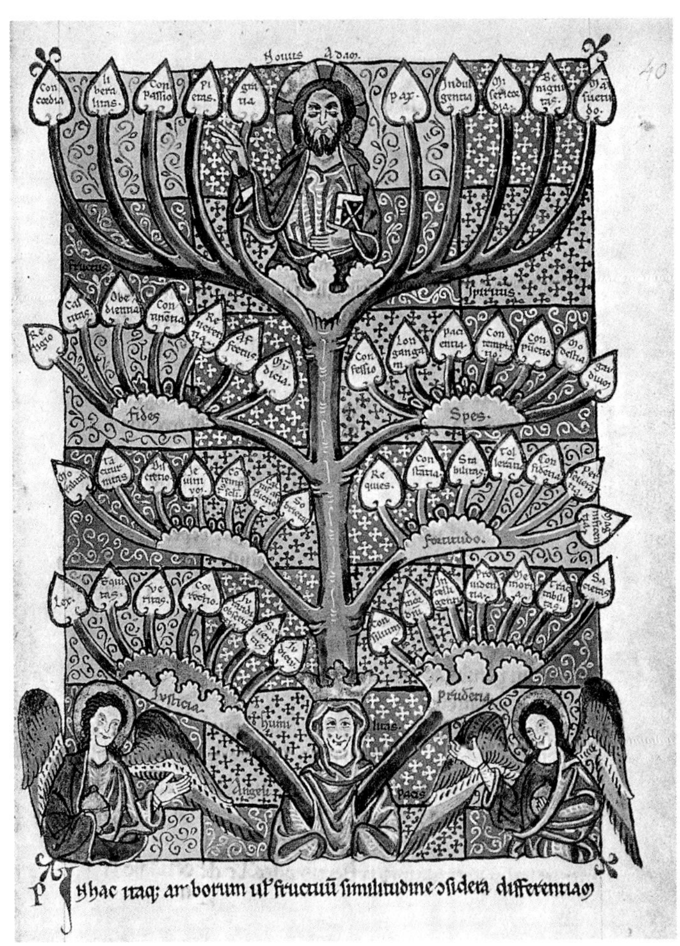

Tree of Virtues from the *Speculum Virginum*

The Symbolism of the Tree

Even the recognition of relatively straightforward meanings and allusions — such as the symbolic connection between the fruit-bearing tree and the future mother who will ensure the future of the family — presupposes certain modes of perception. In fact this raises the question as to whether a viewer from that time period ("the periode eye"[45]) would have recognized the significance of the picture's various arrangements, associations and attributes — that is, whether the connection between the fruit-bearing orange tree and Flora would have made sense to those for whom the picture was painted. In fact, in the profane iconography developed for Lorenzo the Magnificent, there is at least one example of a formally comparable, significant link between a figure and a tree. On the reverse side of a portrait medallion of Lorenzo the Magnificent, attributed to Niccolò Fiorentino, there is a seated female figure, who personifies the city of Florence [46] (see p. 58). The inscription "Florentia" reveals the woman's identity, and she is clearly under the protection of Lorenzo the Magnificent, for the latter is portrayed — symbolically — as a laurel tree (*lauro nobilis*) apparently growing out of the female figure's back, and protectively sheltering her with its branches. The surrounding inscription (*Tutela Patri[a]e*) also confirms Lorenzo the Magnificent as the "protector of the fatherland" — of Florence. Yet, at the same time, the direct link between the tree-trunk (which does not touch the ground) and Florentia's back brings to mind another thought, namely Lorenzo's "roots" in Florence, his *patria* (native town) which he is seeking to protect. This combination of a symbolic tree and an allegorical female figure is certainly comparable with the principle underlying the significant connection between Flora and the orange tree in Botticelli's *La Primavera*.

The profane iconography of the Renaissance was often formally similar to Christian iconography, for Christian imagery had a tradition going back hundreds of years, and artists were bound to rely on it. This may be seen, for example, in the portraits of women painted in the late fifteenth and early sixteenth centuries which drew heavily on conventional representations of the Madonna,[47] since the Virgin Mary was regarded as the model for every woman and mother. These comparisons

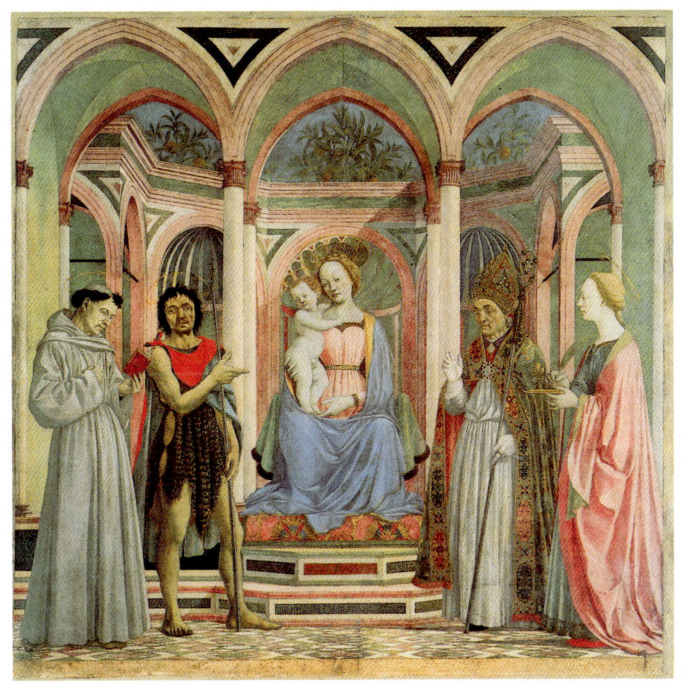

Domenico Veneziano
Madonna and Child with Saints
(Altarpiece for S. Lucia de' Magnoli), c. 1445

to the Madonna paid tribute to her exemplary role among women. Similar links between sacred and profane iconography are also found in representations of trees and of orange trees.[48] In addition, Christian iconography throws light on the associations that an orange tree, or any tree, can evoke if portrayed with a female figure. In representations of the Madonna, the orange tree was taken as a reference to the immaculate conception or as an allusion to paradise. In medieval manuscripts such as the *Liber floridus* or the *Speculum Virginum,* Mary, as the *radix virtutum* (root of virtue), was shown directly linked to the Tree of Virtue, creating an immediate connection with the Mother of God and the tree growing out of her body[49] (see p. 59). Certain Christian symbols could be transferred to profane iconography: a tree represented the virtuous qualities of a bride. Among trees of virtue and of life, the orange tree

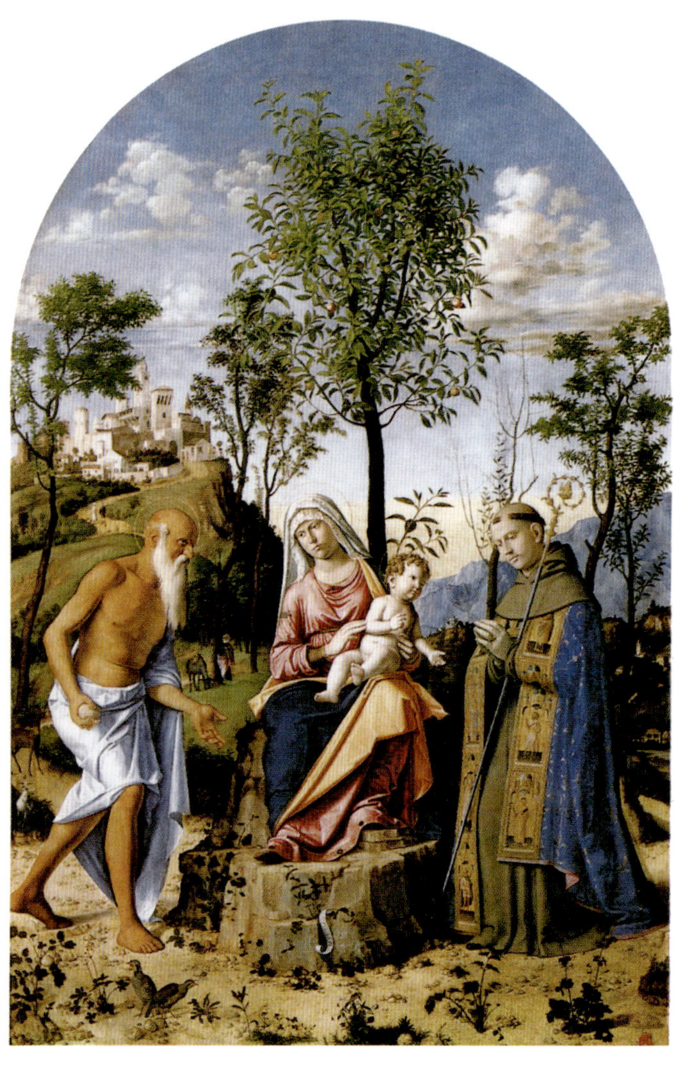

Cima da Conegliano
Madonna and Child with Saints (Madonna dell'Arancio), 1496

in particular with its fruits and blossoms (sometimes also the lemon tree) frequently appears behind the throne of the Madonna in numerous Italian Renaissance altarpieces.[50] The visual link between the orange tree and the Mother of God, as it had already been established in medieval manuscripts, is found in altarpiece paintings showing the so-called *sacra conversazione,* a genre which was introduced in Florence around 1445 by Domenico Veneziano's painting for the church of Santa Lucia de' Magnoli[51] (see p. 61). Here an orange tree, half hidden by the Madonna's throne, is directly related to Mary's body. In its crown it has the orange-red, glowing fruits evoking thoughts of paradise and the promise of salvation. The link between Mary and the orange tree is more clearly portrayed in Venetian altarpieces, such as Cima da Conegliano's *Madonna and Child with Saints (Madonna dell' Arancio)*,[52] painted in 1496. This work reflects an older version of the motif — one which no doubt also served as a model for Domenico Veneziano and which was closely related in its iconography to the aforementioned medieval representations of the tree of virtue. In the middle of this large-scale altarpiece, the Virgin Mary, gently inclined to the left, sits enthroned in front of a landscape. The tree does not seem to be growing out of the rocky ground on which Mary is sitting with the Christ-Child; instead it seems to be growing from between the two figures. Together, Mary, the Child and the tree form a trinity, strengthened on the right side by a young branch which in turn seems to be growing out of the head of the Child. The viewer would certainly grasp the connection between the fruit of the Madonna's womb and the fruit-bearing tree.

The examples used for comparison here can of course not be viewed as iconographic models, yet they played their part in determining the conventions of "seeing" at the time and pave the way for some important observations regarding Botticelli's *La Primavera*. The contemporary viewer was just as familiar with symbolic combinations of woman and tree as with the symbolism linking the Medici family with oranges and with laurels. In broader terms, these same symbols also stood for marriage, the family, motherhood and the advent of future generations.

For all those involved in *La Primavera* — Lorenzo the Magnificent who commissioned it, the bride and groom to whom it was addressed, and the Medici's humanist adviser (probably Angelo Poliziano) — a work such as this presented an opportunity to draw widely on art and learning to create an ideal pictorial world that would be of relevance to the newly-married couple. And in the process, fragments of text were brought together that were otherwise apparently not connected. For example, Ovid's *Fasti,* a poetic calendar of elegiac distichs, have little in common with Lucretius's *De rerum natura,* a philosophic didactic poem in epic hexameters, or with Virgil's *Aeneid,* a monumental epic, or with the odes of Horace. This textual heterogeneity and the fragmentary nature of the texts involved is still felt in the arrangement of the figures, standing in a row in front of a dark background and seemingly isolated from one another.

At the left edge of the composition, Mercury is disinterestedly turning away from the rest of the scene and only concerned with the trails of mist which he actually ought to be dispersing with somewhat greater determination. In view of his rather hesitant prodding at the wintry clouds, one is bound to wonder whether winter is really so easy to drive away. The Three Graces appear more dynamic, and yet each is self-absorbed and they are for the most part looking past each other, perfectly indifferent to what is happening around them. The more inviting figure of Venus — although she is perhaps only inviting observation rather than participation — is totally isolated from the events in the rest of the scene. Zephyrus and Chloris are entirely wrapped up in each other and are thus equally isolated, as though cut off in

Venus,
the goddess of love

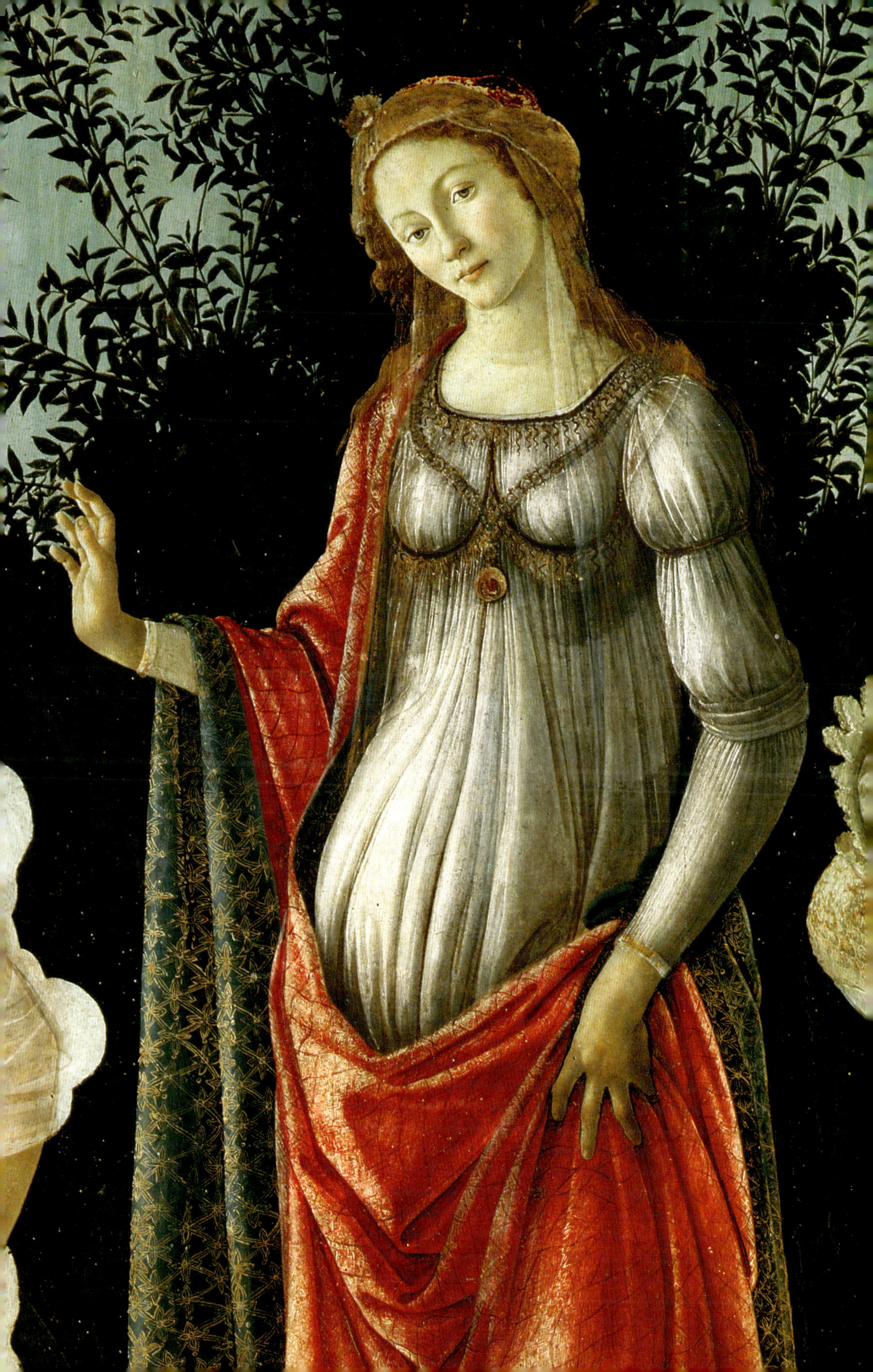

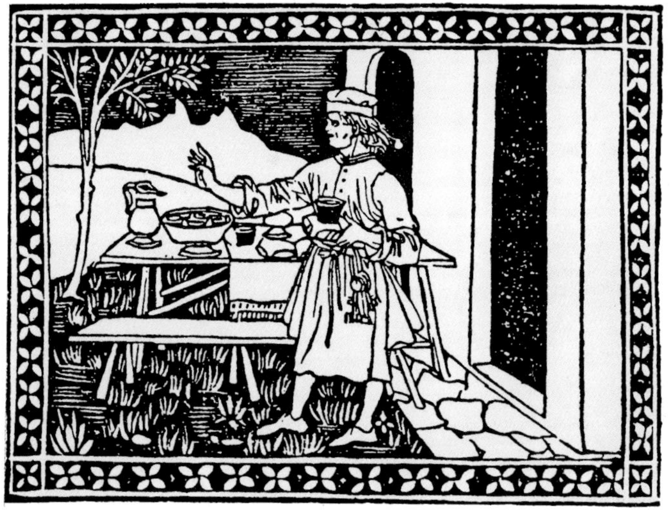

Woodcut illustration from Jacobus de Cessoli's *Libro di giuocho degli scacchi*, 1493/94

their own sphere of operation, which the artist has emphasized in the noticeably bent trees at the right edge of the picture as opposed to the static trees and plants in the rest of the picture space. And even here, where two characters are involved with each other, there is no harmony, for the nymph is attempting to flee from the pale, faintly bluish god.

The assumption that the figures depicted here have yet to come together — as a bridal couple — is strengthened if one considers the historical facts at the time the painting was made. The marriage between Lorenzo and Semiramide was not a love match: on the contrary, it was purely a political undertaking painstakingly planned by Lorenzo the Magnificent. After the Pazzi Conspiracy in 1478 and the subsequent disturbances, the Medici were excommunicated by the Pope and, as a result, were largely isolated politically in Italy. In order to counter this isolation, in 1479 Lorenzo the Magnificent set about improving the family's political relations with the powerful Aragonesi family in Naples, who were allies of the Pope.

In 1480 his political situation was further strengthened by the commencement of negotiations regarding a marriage between Lorenzo di Pierfrancesco and Semiramide Appiani.

The Appiani family had already been connected by marriage with the Aragonesi since the previous generation. They controlled the most important Tuscan harbor, Piombiono, as well as the iron ore mines on Elba, and were viewed as the ideal partners for Florence and the Medici, who were concerned to gain access to shipping routes and secure permanent concessions to mine iron ore. Thus, a firm connection through marriage with the Appiani family would be most useful to Lorenzo the Magnificent in achieving political aims.[53] In the matter of this politically-motivated marriage, the young couple, as yet still minors, were of necessity passive participants and therefore the magic of the painting itself was directed first and foremost towards them: it was to convince them of their own marriage — which may have been particularly necessary in the case of the bride.

Botticelli's depiction of Chloris being taken by force, inspired by Ovid's description, corresponded to the politically-motivated, arranged marriage which took little account of the personal feelings and needs of the bride. In this sense one could see the painting as a form of compensation for the distinctly unromantic circumstances of the wedding, for the luxurious wealth of flowers reflects perfectly Ovid's portrayal of Flora's situation: "Goddess, be queen of flowers." The inviting gesture of Venus, recognizable in book illustrations of that period (see p. 66), may here be understood as a welcoming gesture to the bride, even as a command to enter the realm of love and of spring, and to take up her role as its mistress (see p. 65).

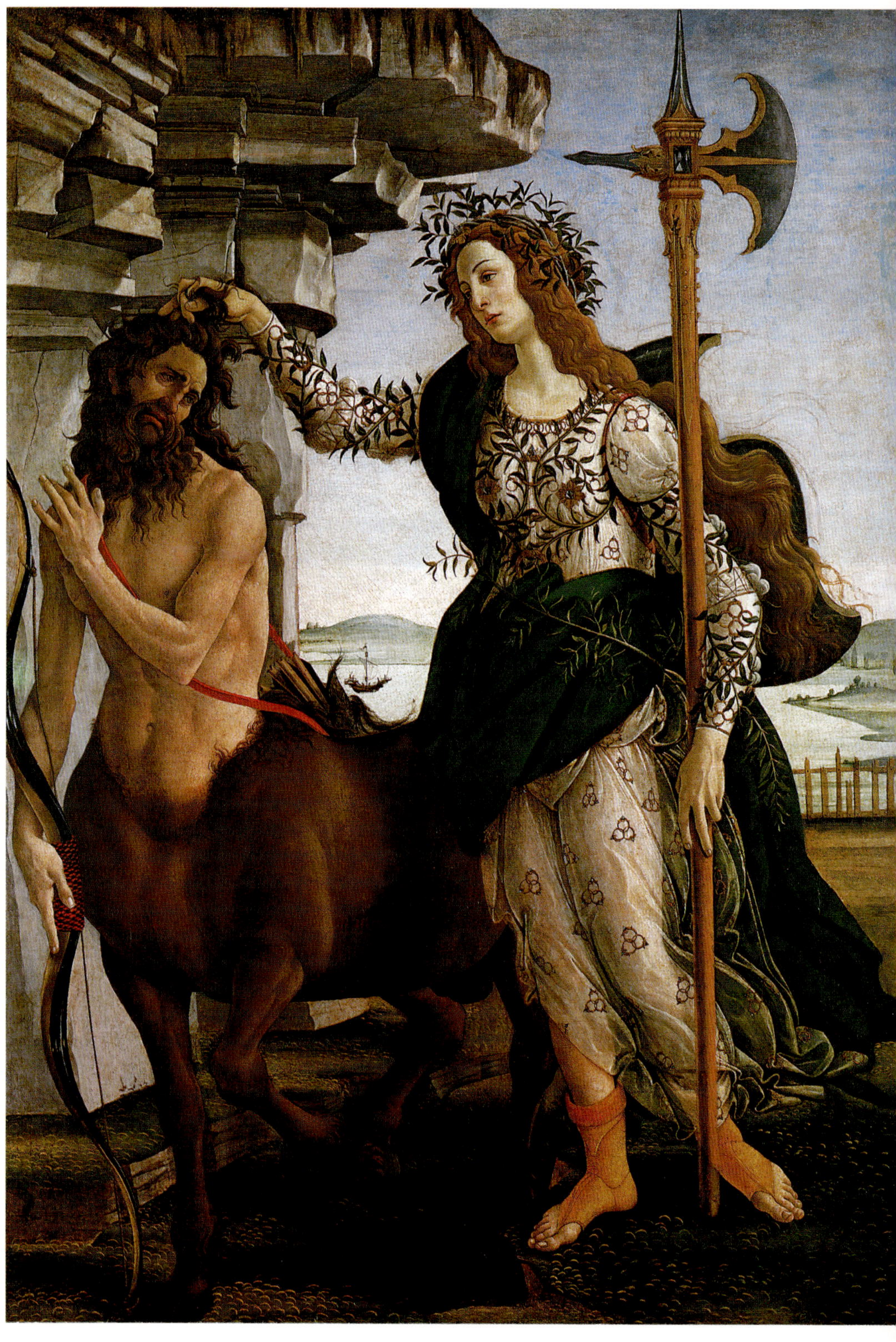

Minerva and the Centaur: An Image of Feminine Domination

While the eclectic combination of figures in Botticelli's *La Primavera* should be understood as a consequence of the artist's use of a variety of sources and the historical circumstances surrounding the picture's creation, the elegance of the central figures — the Graces, Venus and Flora — expresses the promise of the same love and marital harmony which Ovid described as making amends for the violence done to Chloris. This sense of redress, from the bride's point of view, is taken up again in Botticelli's *Minerva and the Centaur.* This work hung above a door, to the left of *La Primavera,* and was thus part of the same furnishings and decorations in the bride's chamber.[54] In contrast to *La Primavera,* where the whole right side of the picture is devoted to the taking of the bride and the question of masculine dominance, *Minerva and the Centaur* portrays the taming of a male monster, in this case a centaur. In front of a landscape, cut off to the left by overhanging rocks, we see a hybrid creature with the lower body of an animal and the lighter coloured upper-body of a human being. The wildness of the rugged rocks in the middle ground corresponds to the wild, unruly appearance of the legendary being. Yet the centaur — despite his bow and a quiver full of arrows — does not seem to be harboring warlike intentions, because his arrows are safely in their quiver and, as we can see the bow is slack. This fiend, turning away disconsolately rather than displaying any overt aggression, is completely under the control of a mythological figure, identifiable as Minerva, who gently holds him by a lock of his hair.

Minerva and the Centaur, c. 1482–83

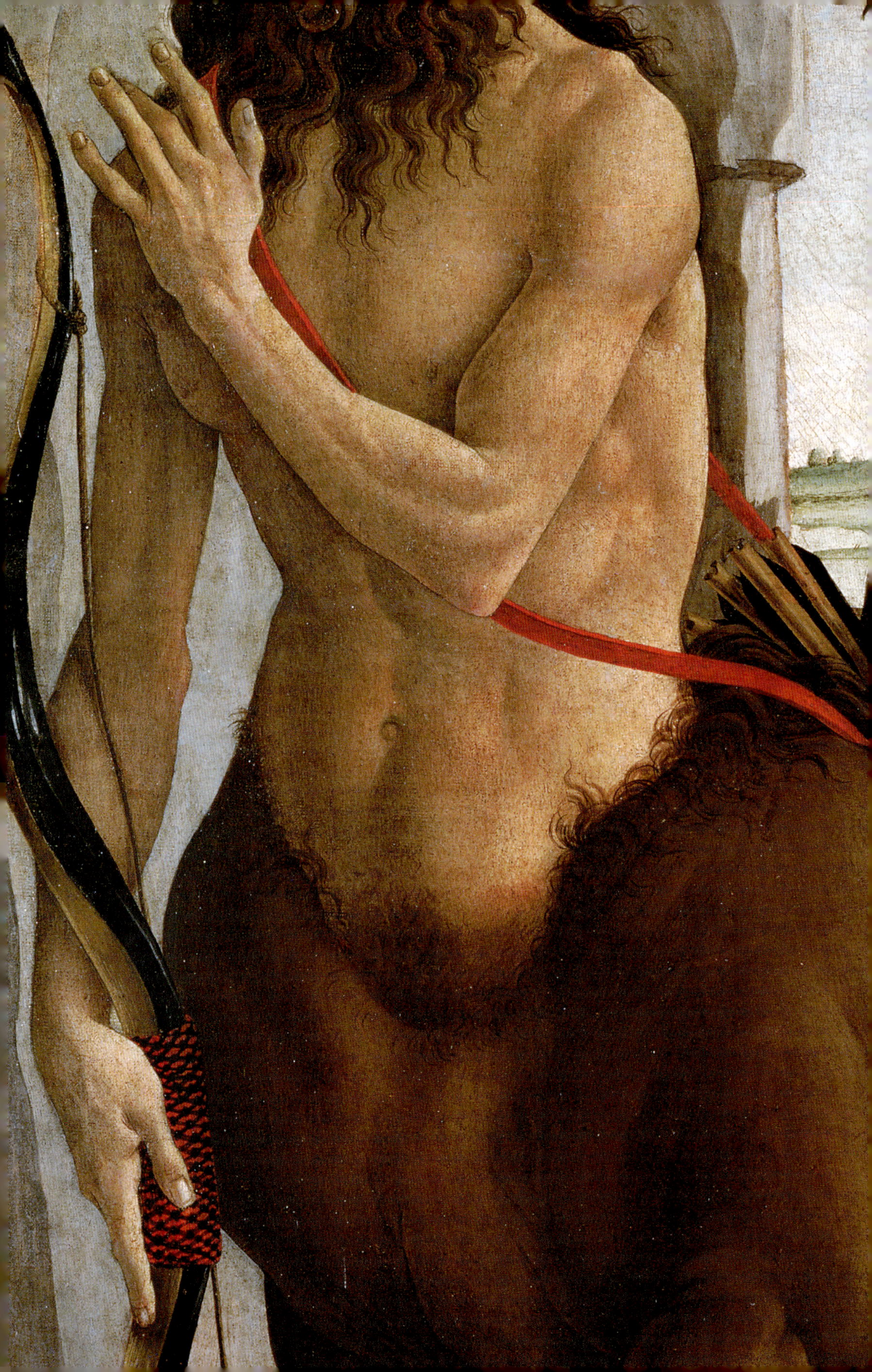

With her halberd, she is more heavily armed than he and thus, presumably, also more dangerous than the monster.

The mythological centaur, with its bestial lower half, is the embodiment of fleshly lust unrestrained by any moderating conventions. In classical accounts, he is portrayed as wild and violent. In medieval mythological manuscripts the centaur becomes the incarnation of unbridled sexual desire per se: "Centaurs, namely, who are said to be half human and half horse, personify (Latin text: *denotant*) such men whose fleshly lust has turned them into beasts."[55] A sense of those bestial qualities is conveyed by the darkly colored, animalistic lower body with the genitals clearly in view as a sign of male aggression and sexuality. Next to the figure stands Minerva, the personification of wisdom, who — simply because she is so virtuous — is in a position to tame the evil, animal-like behaviour of the other. As a sign of her power and victory over the lasciviousness personified in the centaur, she takes hold of his head as though it were completely separate from his lower half, and thus entirely in her power. Yet Minerva not only appears as an agent for the regulating of carnal desire as she meets it in the shape of the centaur; she may also serve as an opposing figure to Amor in the neighboring painting *La Primavera*. The blind, and thus uncontrollable son of Venus was a symbol of sensual pleasure (*voluptas*), similar to the centaur,[56] while the chase Minerva was regarded as a restraining counter-balance to the cheeky little rogue.

The theme of feminine dominance, as it emerges here, is identifiable in other, usually smaller, picture types from that time period. Typical of these were the *deschi da parto* — salvers which were ordered for the occasion of a birth and presented to the mother. These were frequently decorated with more or less extravagant depictions of the

The slack bow of the centaur

Triumph of Love, often shown as a ceremonial horse-drawn carriage accompanied by festively-dressed figures. In an example from the mid-fifteenth century, a figure of Amor stands in the centre, armed with a flaming bow and arrow and supported by three smaller cherubs who are eagerly releasing their weapons of love[57] (see p. 74). Yet, more interesting in fact than the activities of Amor and his cohorts is the scene in the lower half of the work where two men are being mistreated by two women: Aristotle by Phyllis and Samson by Delilah. Phyllis was the beautiful mistress of Alexander the Great, and Aristotle was Alexander's teacher for a time. After the philosopher had warned the ruler against the detrimental influence of beautiful women on able men, the enraged — and now vengeful — Phyllis kindled such burning desire in the old man that, in order to prove his love, he was prepared to serve her as a beast of burden. And so the woman proved her power over the great philosopher. Power is also the central issue in the story of Delilah, who cut off the mighty Samson's hair and, so it was said, by this act completely robbing him of all his strength.[58] Thus the lower half of the commemorative salver demonstrates the triumph of women over the intellectual (Aristotle) and the physical (Samson) strength of man. On the occasion of a birth, a female-"dominated" event, it was customary to order a *desco da parto* which depicted men temporarily subjugated by women. A comparable visual image — although not (yet) relating to a birth — is conveyed in the figure of the centaur in Botticelli's picture, for despite his physical superiority and his legendary wildness, he has been robbed of his power by the female personification of virtue and has thus been tamed. The unstable position of his head may also be interpreted in this same sense. In

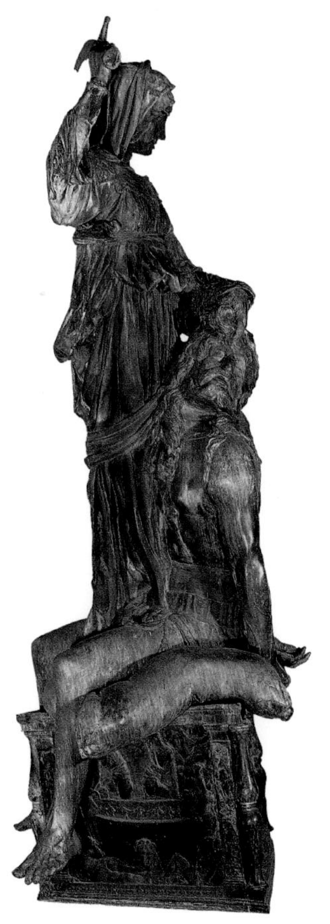

Donatello
Judith and Holofernes, c. 1456

Right: Head of the centaur

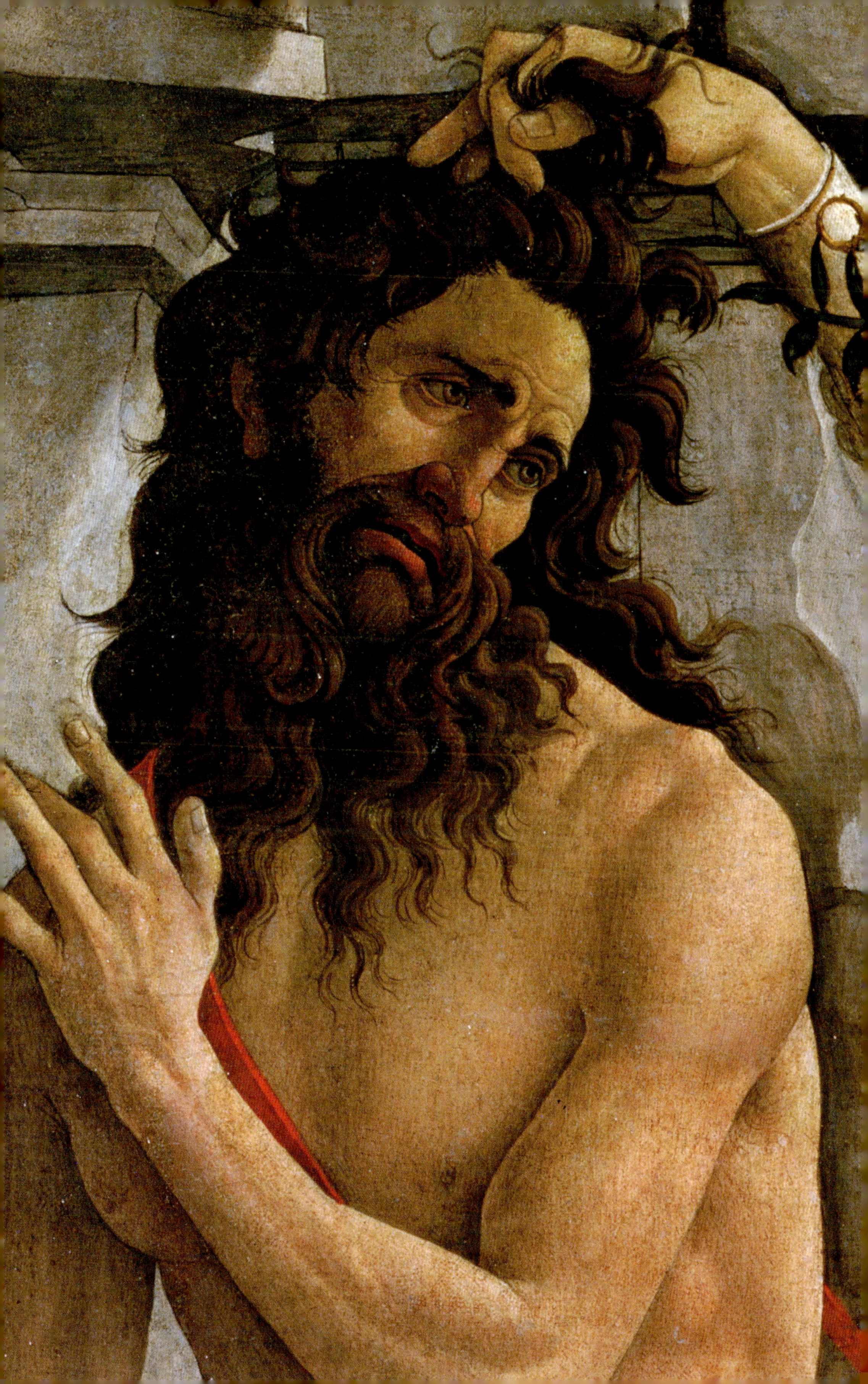

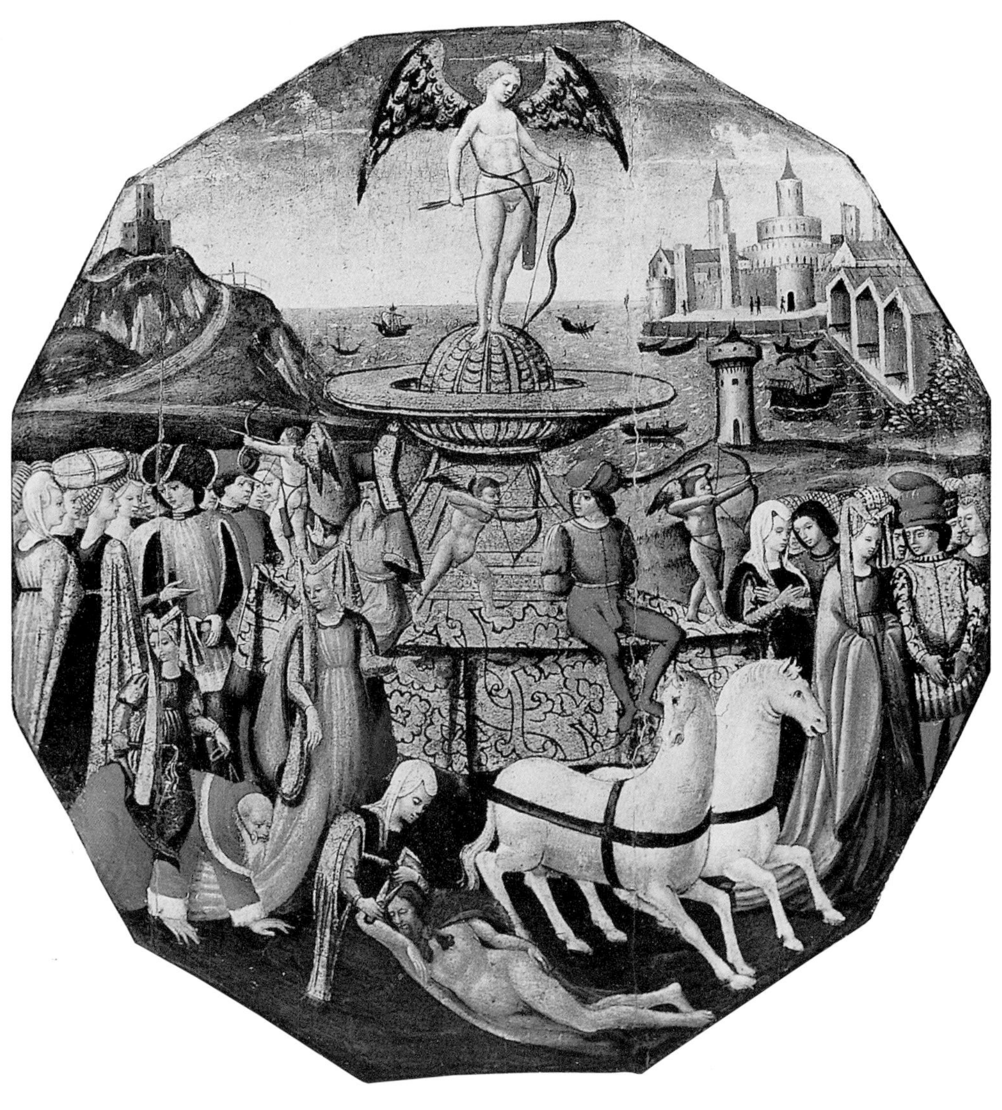

Workshop of Apollonio di Giovanni, birth salver showing the *Triumph of Love*

formal terms, the head of the centaur, somewhat disconnected from his body, is reminiscent of contemporary depictions of Judith, who either during or immediately after the decapitation of Holofernes leaves the detached head resting on the torso of the conquered general. A comparable formal arrangement, for example, to that in Botticelli's painting may be found in Donatello's *Judith and Holofernes.* A widely accepted interpretation of this bloody event is the triumph of the virtue of humility, embodied as Judith, over the vice of pride, which Holofernes is sometimes taken to represent.[59] Here too, as in Botticelli's painting, virtue in the shape of a woman triumphs over vice in the form of a man. Formal parallels between the sculpture and the painting may not be due to chance, but may be due to the fact that the two works share the same theme, the triumph of virtue over vice.

Despite the fact that virtue is triumphant in this picture, Botticelli's Minerva does not at first appear to be an energetic and dominating person. Instead she seems to be looking out into the world somewhat dreamily. Her right arm seems almost powerless, and she grasps the centaur's matted hair with tenderness rather than with determination. Thus it is clear that feminine dominance is by no means a consequence of bodily power and its decisive application, but derives instead from other characteristics which Botticelli conveys to the viewer with the help of decorative elements rich in symbolism. Thus Minerva's entire upper body, hair, and arms are entwined with olive shoots as a symbol of feminine virtue. The same meaning is conveyed in the numerous diamond rings on her dress and the over-sized diamond at the top end of her halberd. Because of their indestructible hardness and crystalline clarity, diamonds were also regarded as a symbol of virtue. Thus it is by her virtue that the woman dominates the lasciviousness that she is confronted with in the figure of the centaur; this is the moral underlying the scene. At the same time, Minerva is also portrayed as an ideal role model for the bride; this is indicated by the symbolism of the diamond rings, a symbol for the Medici family. Since the artist has covered the dress of Minerva with symbols of the groom's family, this indicates her as an ideal image for the bride.[60]

The sight of Minerva with her halberd and her symbolic embellishments, standing as the guardian of virtue above the door of the bridal chamber, also explains the unusual direction that *La Primavera* (placed to its right) should be read in. The picture of spring has to be read from right to left, and not from left to right as might otherwise be expected. When the painting is "read" in this manner, the following sequence emerges: Zephyrus, alias Lorenzo di Pierfrancesco as the groom, hunts and overpowers the virginal nymph who becomes his bride by being abducted and losing her innocence. Thus, as Ovid's text suggests, the groom abducts his bride Semiramide Appiani alias Chloris alias Flora into the realm of chaste Venus, who stands with a gesture of welcome more or less in the centre of the picture. Semiramide is the mistress of this realm of flower-laden fertility; here she and her spouse will bring forth their desired offspring. Her chaste fertility is underlined by the presence of the Three Graces. The temporary closure of this sequence is represented by Mercury, alias Lorenzo the Magnificent, who disperses the winter winds and thus creates a climate favorable to marriage and fertility. He turns away from the scene portrayed in the first picture and leads the way into the contrapuntal companion piece, namely the taming of the centaur by Minerva, an image of feminine domination which focuses on the motif of the domestication of unbridled masculine desire by a virtuous woman.

In view of the circumstances surrounding the painting of *La Primavera* and its "counter-image," we have drawn the conclusion that the original intention was that these two paintings should convince the newly-married couple of their own wedding. It is precisely this didactic intention — for the purposes of persuasion —

Minerva entwined in olive shoots

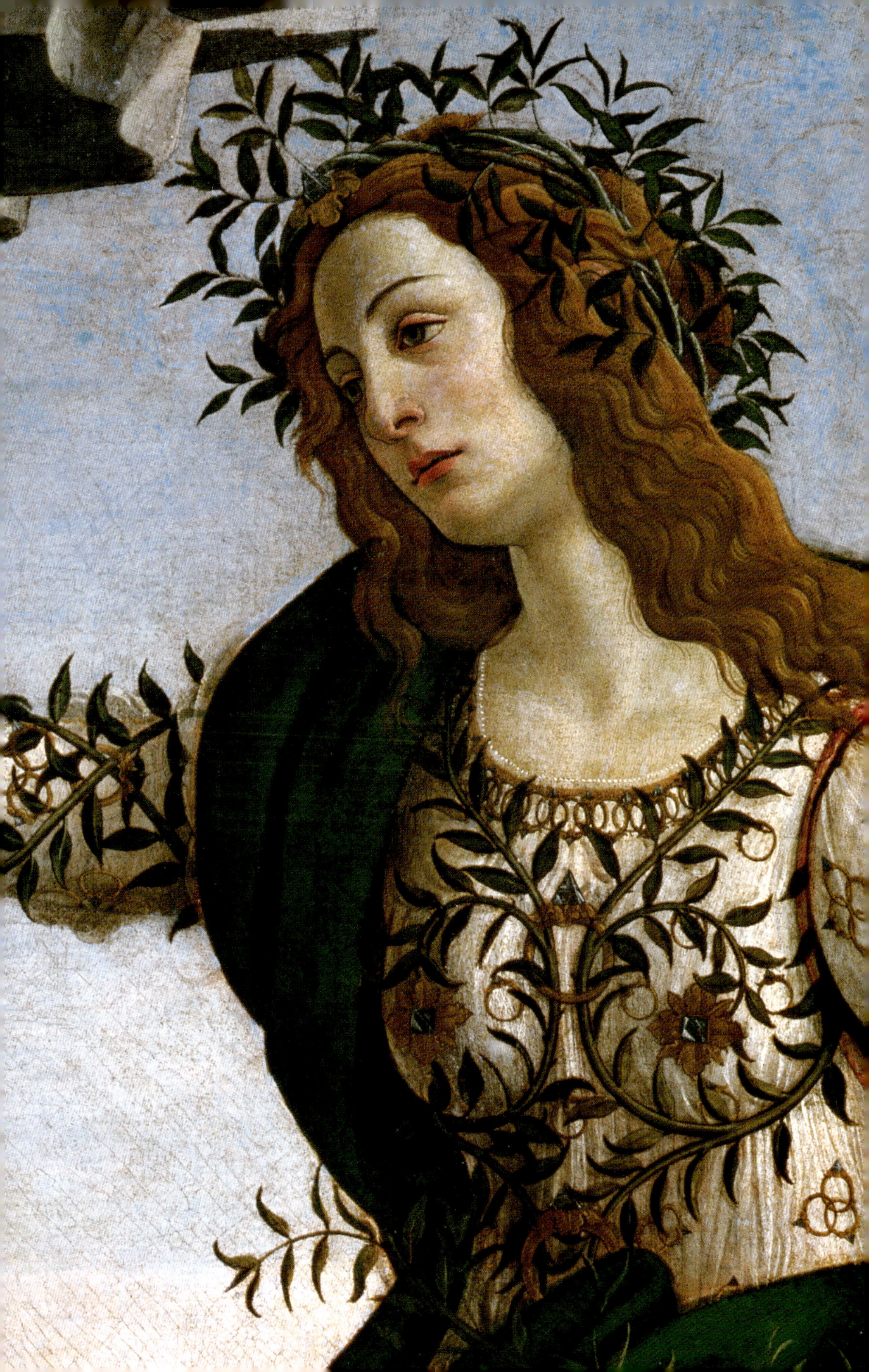

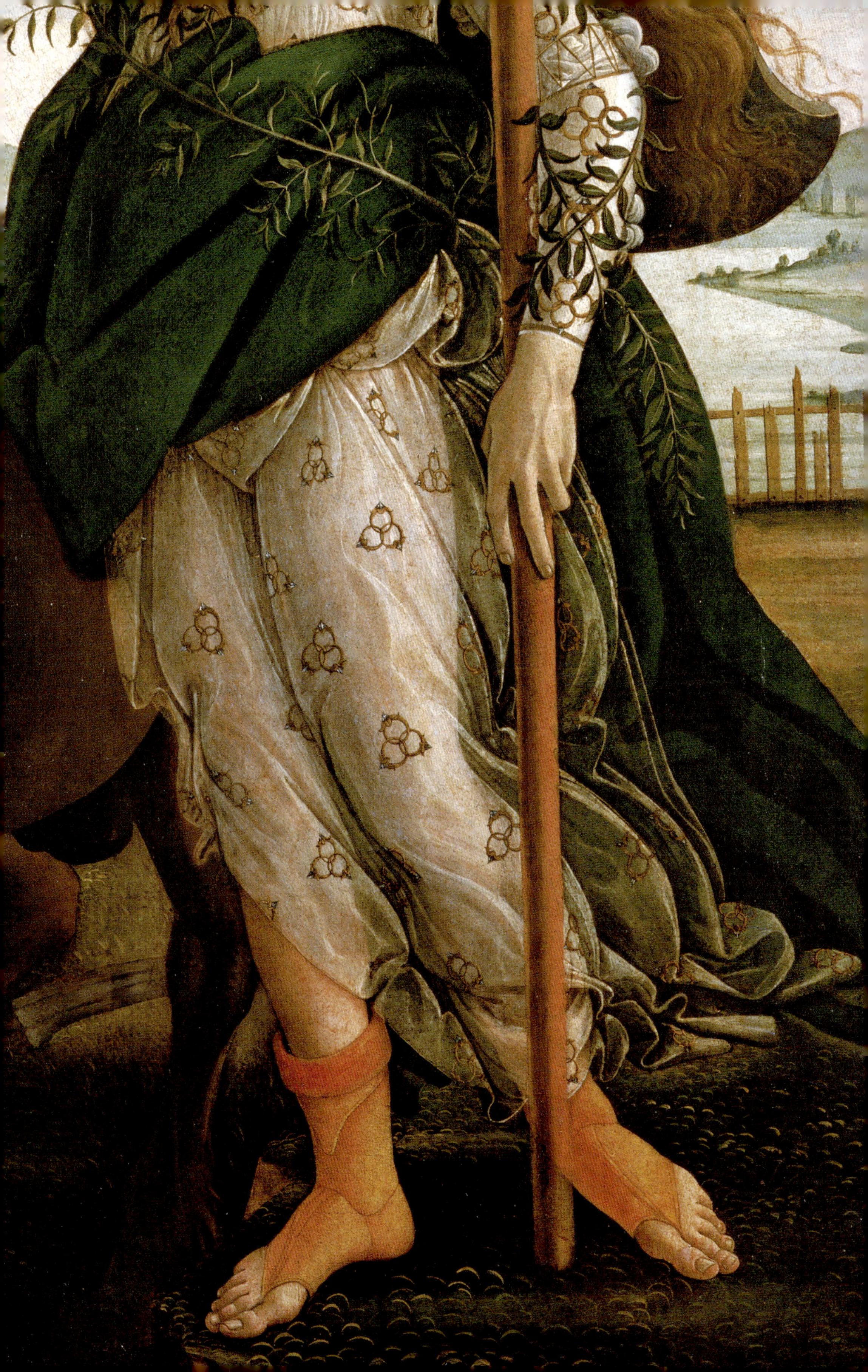

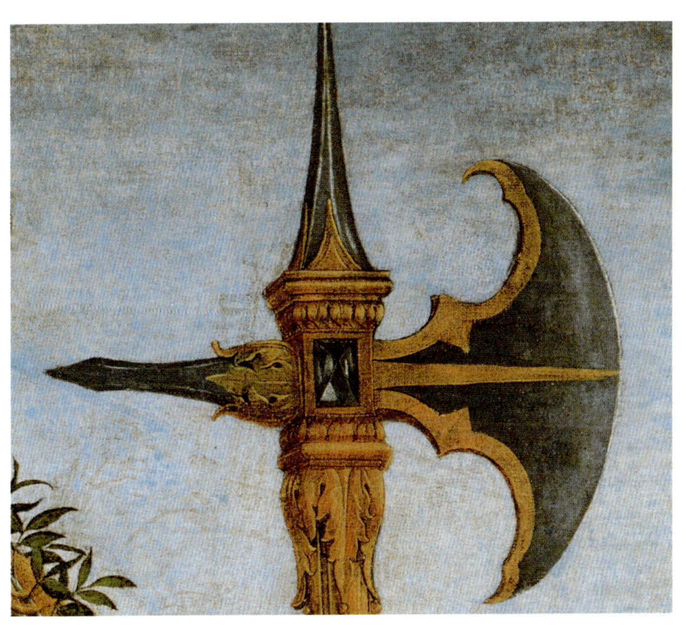

that is touched on in the previously cited letter written by Marsilio Ficino to Lorenzo the Magnificent, in which the Medici's "resident" humanist talks of painted beauty as an encouragement to virtue and love and, in doing so, describes the ideal effect of painting. Beyond the intended didacticism of the images, however, yet another desired result may have motivated the displaying of these two mythological paintings. *La Primavera* hung in a bed chamber above the bride's bed and there — if one views this as Botticelli's contemporaries would have done — it would have had a direct influence on the bride's fertility. In *On Building*, Leon Battista Alberti, whose tract *On Painting* we have already cited, describes the potentially stimulating decoration of private rooms and bed chambers: "Wherever man and wife come together, it is advisable only to hang portraits of [persons] of dignity and handsome appearance, for they say that this may have a great influence on the fertility of the mother and the appearance of future offspring."[61]

Minerva's gown decorated with diamond rings

Above: Diamond set into Minerva's halberd

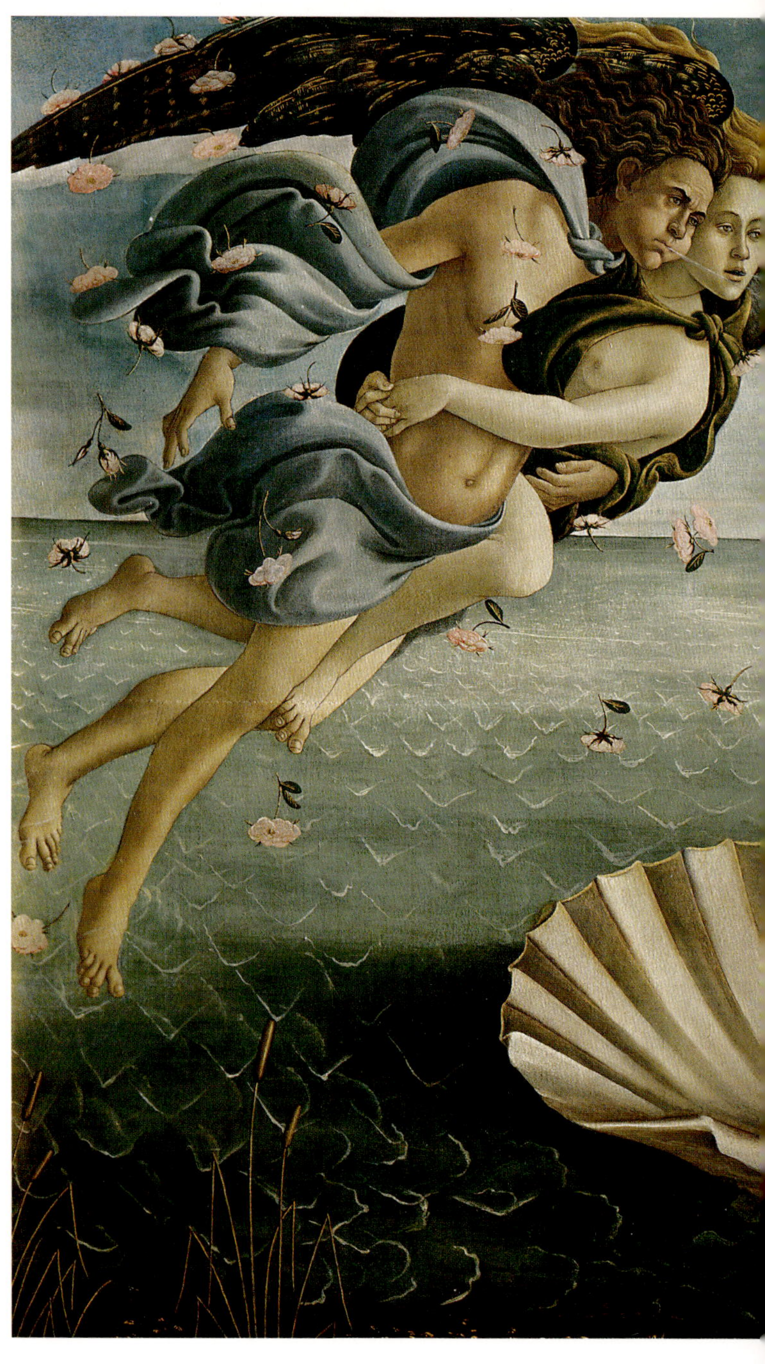

The Birth of Venus, c. 1484–86

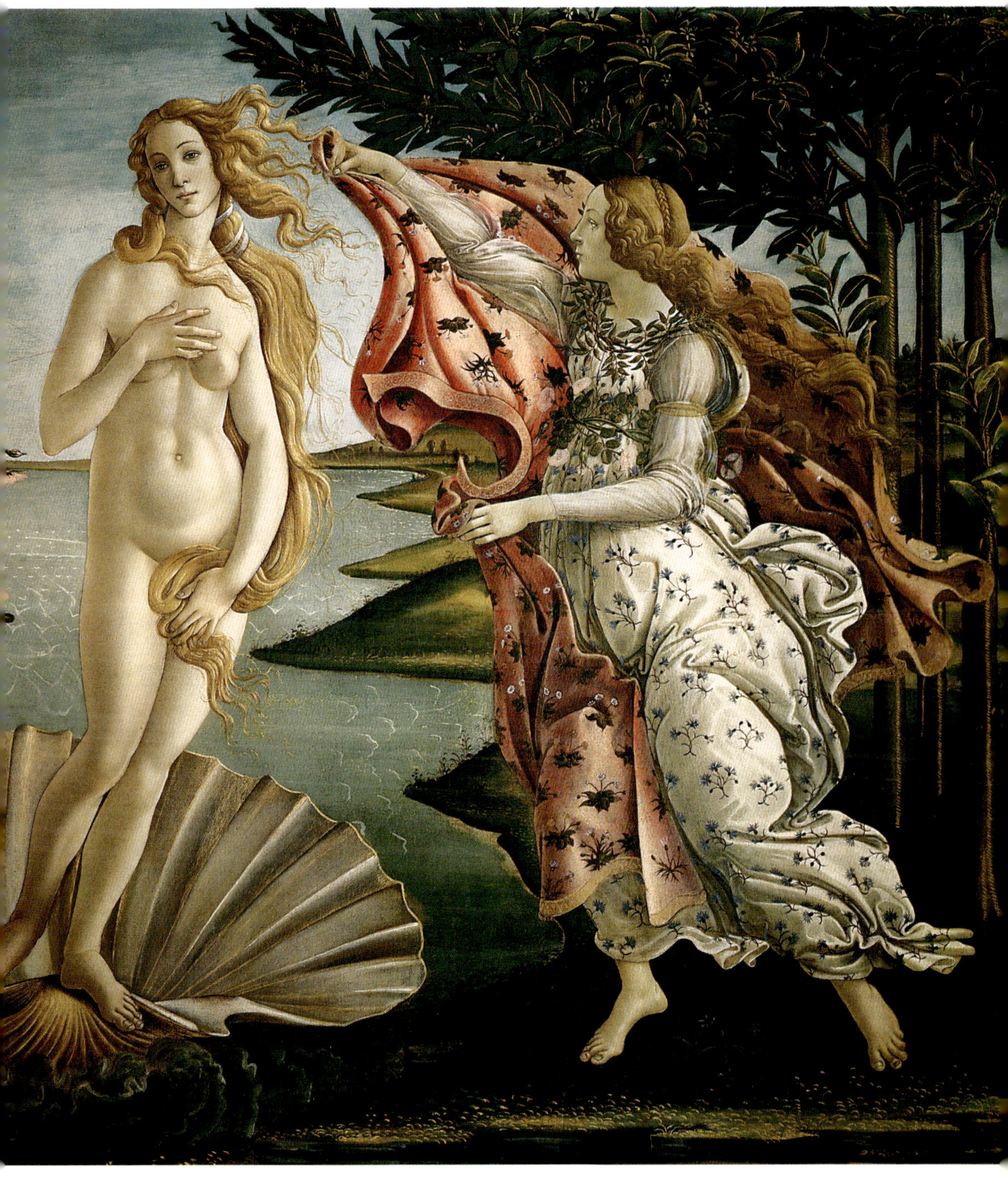

The Birth of Venus: An Image of Arrival

The best known paintings are often the least understood. This certainly applies to another of Botticelli's major works. Today in the Uffizi Gallery in Florence, measuring nearly six-by-nine feet (two-by-three metres), a tempera work on canvas which has become famous as *The Birth of Venus,* is in fact a portrayal of the arrival of the goddess of love at the island of Cyprus. This most famous post-classical depiction of Venus is not as well documented as Botticelli's image of spring. All we know is that in the middle of the sixteenth century *The Birth of Venus,* together with *La Primavera,* was in the possession of descendants of Lorenzo di Pierfrancesco and Giovanni di Pierfrancesco.[62] The work's literary sources have also long been identified, as have its artistic and formal forerunners. However, thus far, few details of the picture have been interpreted either coherently or convincingly. In addition, it is not entirely clear who commissioned the work, although the blossoming orange trees in the background and the previous ownership of the picture would suggest someone from the Medici circle. It is unlikely that a less prominent family in Florence would have commissioned a profane work of this scale.

The composition of this rectangular picture relies on a harmonious, almost axial arrangement of the figures. A female figure in the centre, almost life-size and completely nude — Venus — dominates the picture space. She stands in classical contrapposto in a huge shell which she is evidently using as a ship-like, sea-worthy vessel. She is only partially, yet elegantly, covering her

Venus, the goddess of love

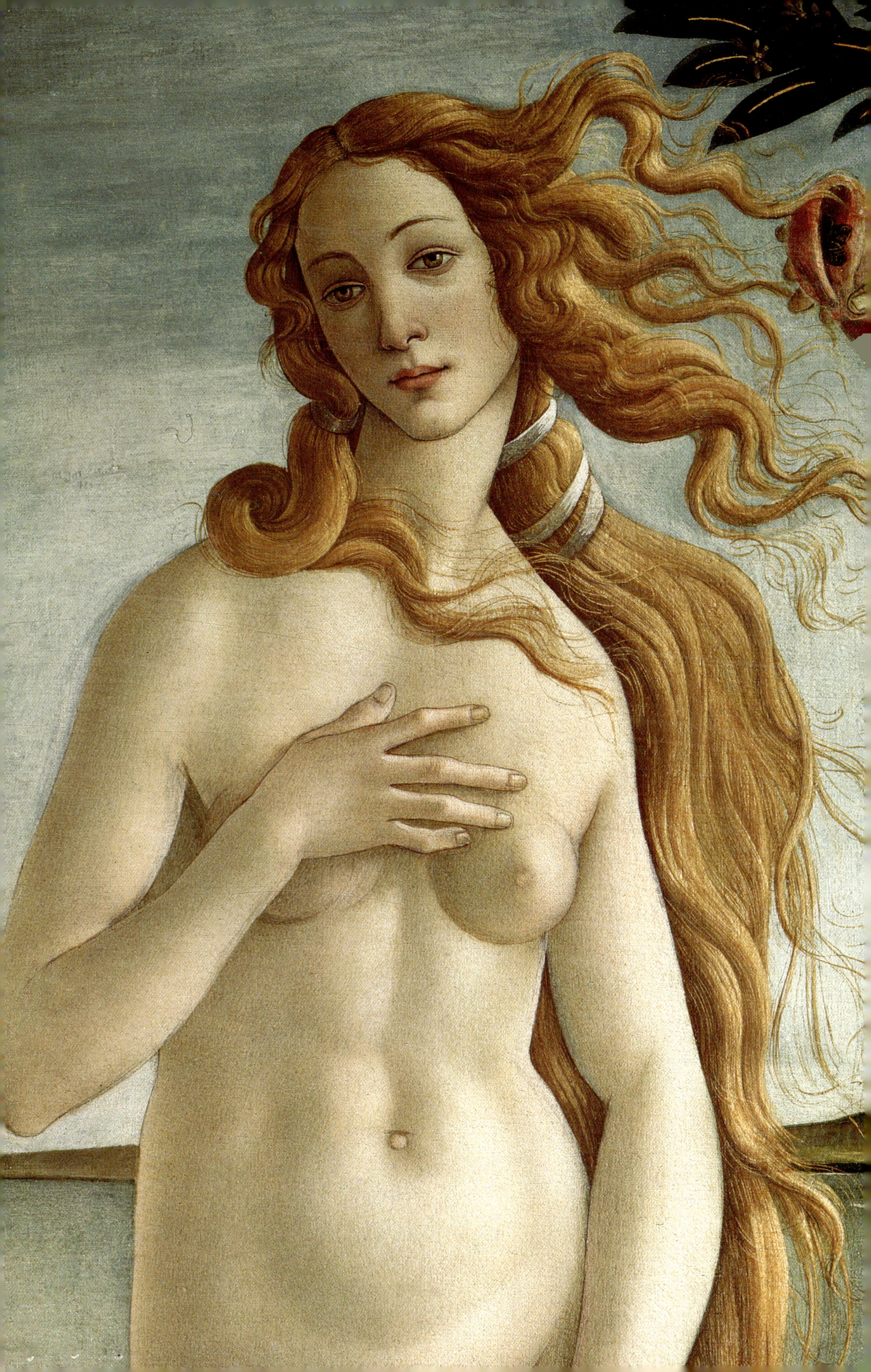

breasts with her lower right arm and hand. With her left hand she is grasping her luxuriant wind-blown hair, discreetly holding it in front of herself. The goddess of love, like an alabaster statue, is flanked by three figures in motion. In the left half of the picture, two figures in the air are floating towards Venus, their nude bodies partially covered by light, fluttering draperies. The figure in front is male, while the figure behind is female. They have their arms around each other and it looks to all appearances as though only the male figure has wings. The most likely interpretation of the male figure is that this is Zephyrus, the warming wind of spring. With his cheeks puffed out, he is creating a current of air which Botticelli painted as a number of fine lines. The female figure at his side is either Chloris, his spouse, or perhaps — as is more likely — the personification of a weaker wind, a soft breeze (Aura), whose opened mouth is releasing a gentle breath of air. Even if the two figures cannot be identified with complete certainty, their function in the picture is perfectly clear; they are creating the wind that is guiding Venus's craft towards the shore.

In the other half of the picture, on the land, a female figure dressed in white is awaiting the arrival of Venus — indeed she is already welcoming the goddess with an inviting gesture of her right arm, which holds up a red cloak. This cloak is decorated with countless daisies, while her own dress is covered with cornflowers. Her body is encircled by roses and around her neckline there are myrtle twigs. This figure may well be one of the goddesses of the seasons, namely the Hora of summer since cornflowers and roses bloom at the beginning of summer while daisies continue throughout the entire warm season.[63] Behind the Hora, right by the seashore, we see the edge of an orange grove and the coastline

The Hora welcomes Venus at the shore

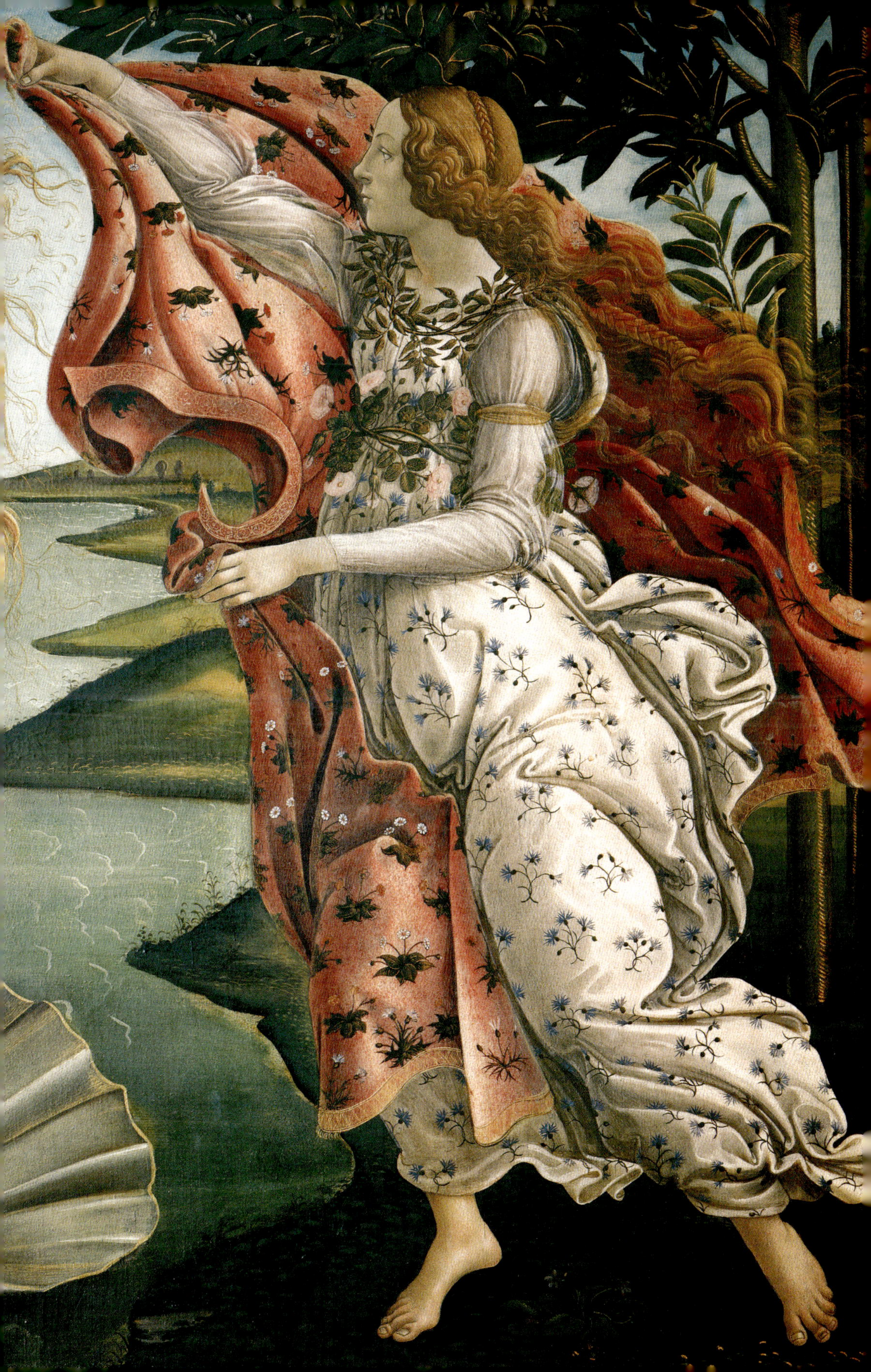

disappearing into the distance in a series of small bays. The three orange trees in the grove have golden-veined leaves and — barely visible — opened blossoms, but no fruits, unlike the trees in *La Primavera*. The rich floral decoration of the Hora is in striking contrast to the

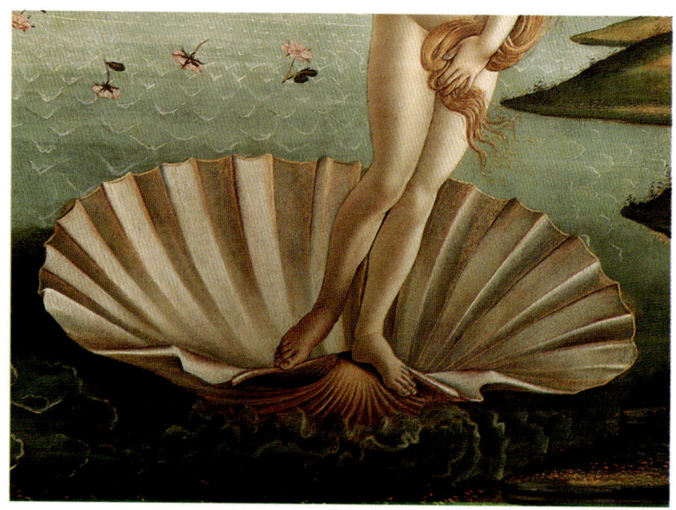

Left: Venus standing in the shell

sparse vegetation of the coastline, which even seems to be made of rock in the bottom right corner of the picture. The evident barrenness of the shore was a deliberate decision on the part of the painter, for here he is basing his portrayal of the scene on Hesiod's *Theogony*. In this, Hesiod writes that it is only when Venus steps onto the land that the flowers bloom and the vegetation comes to life. Thus Botticelli is not only depicting the arrival of Venus but also, more specifically, that moment directly before she stepped onto the shore of Cyprus.[64]

An understanding of the contents of the picture, as in the case of *La Primavera*, is dependent on a knowledge of literary sources which describe a similar situation,

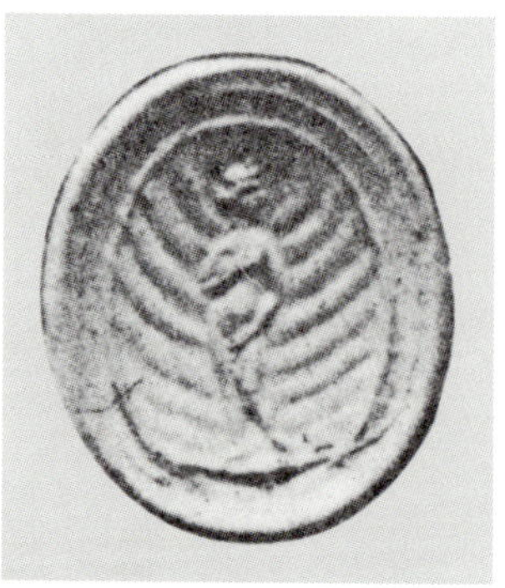

Gemstone depicting Venus in a shell

namely the arrival of Venus gliding across the surface of the sea on a shell, driven by the wind Zephyrus and being welcomed at the shore by the Horae. One particular passage from Homer influenced Botticelli's approach to the subject, in which the arrival of Aphrodite (known as Venus to the Romans) is described in detail:

> Of august gold-wreathed and beautiful Aphrodite
> I shall sing, to whose domain belong the battlements
> of all sea-laved Cyprus where, blown by the moist breath
> of Zephyros,
> she was carried over the waves of the resounding sea
> in soft foam. The gold-filleted Horae
> happily welcomed her and clothed her with heavenly raiment.[65]

As before in Botticelli's *Mars and Venus,* the image only matches the cited description in its general composition, for in Homer's hymn the goddess of love is received by several Horae at once, whereas Botticelli only portrays one. Botticelli may have been given the relevant reference from the Homeric hymns as well as verses from Hesiod's *Theogony* by the court poet to the Medici, Angelo Poliziano, probably in an Italian translation. Poliziano himself, in his *Stanze per la Giostra* (1476–78), had rewritten this passage from the hymns and had given a detailed description of Venus's voyage across the sea. Botticelli was inspired by certain details of this description and adopted them in his own work, such as the shell which is mentioned by Poliziano as the craft in which Venus made her voyage — which is completely absent from the Homeric hymns. This shell was presumably familiar to the poet and his contemporaries from various small-scale classical artworks as well as from classical texts, where it generally emerges as an attribute of Venus and as a symbol meaning many things, including fertility and

Following double-page:
Zephyrus and a nymph, detail from *The Birth of Venus,* c. 1484–86

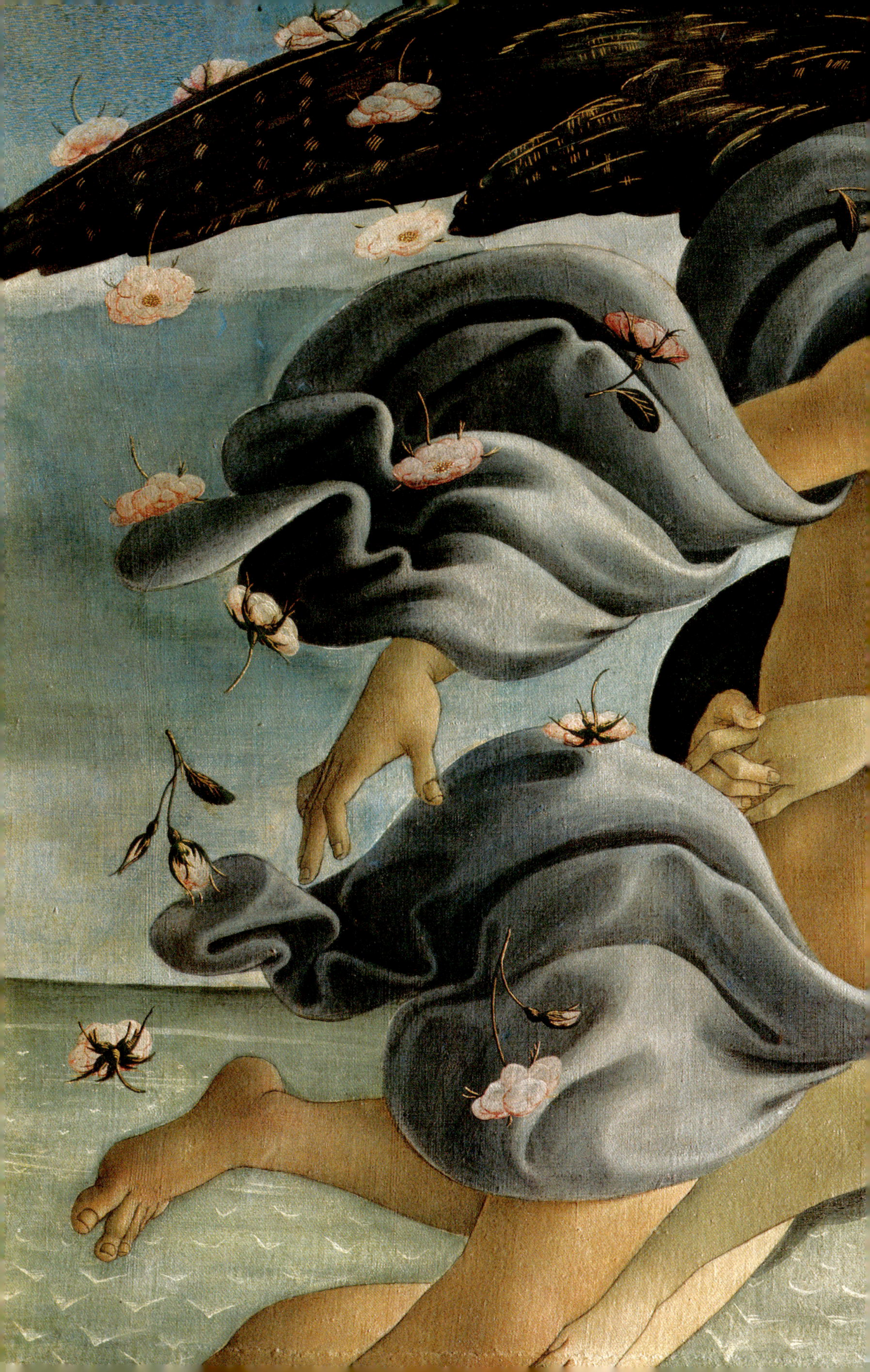

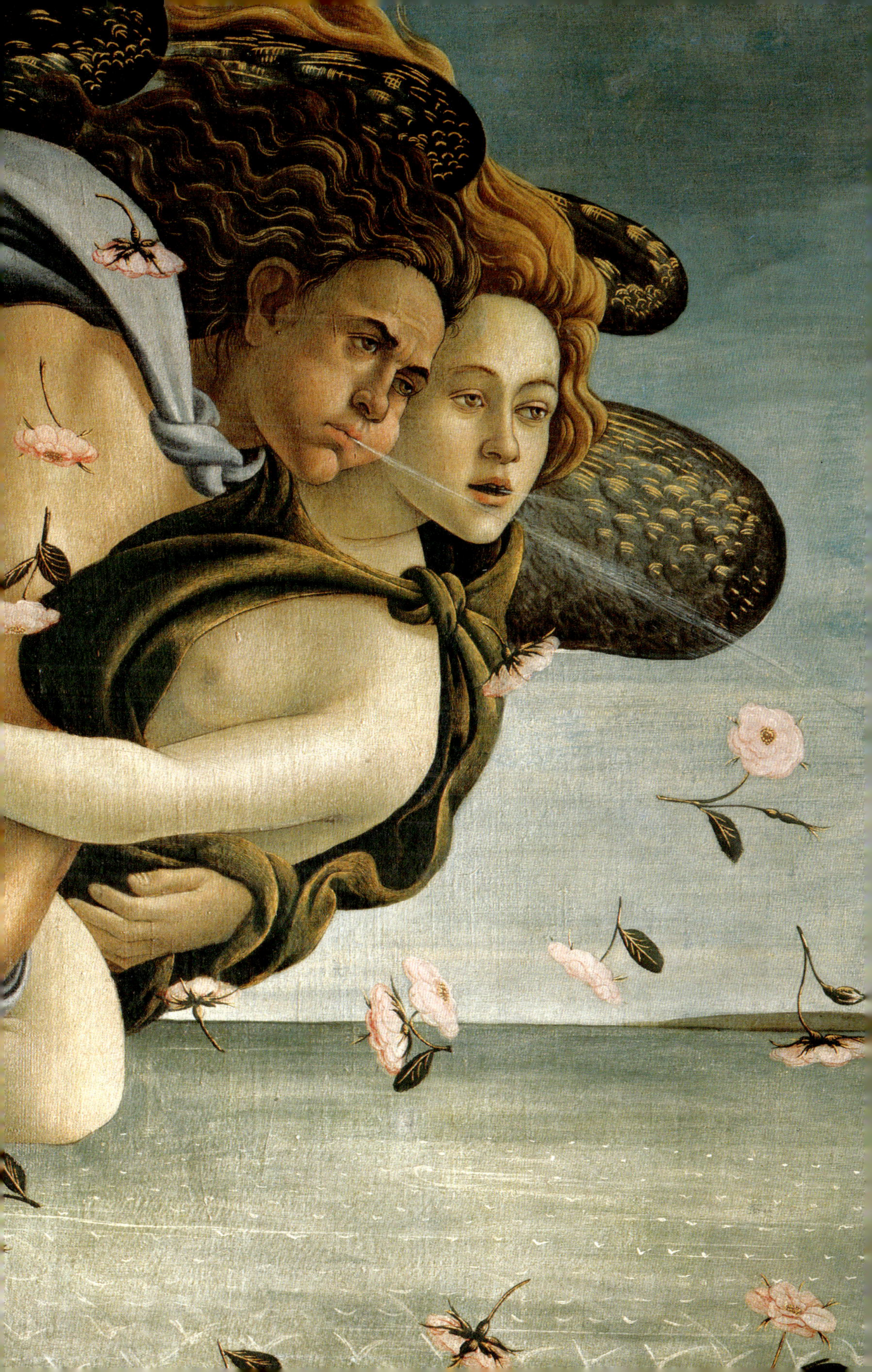

birth.[66] The relevant passage in Poliziano's description of Venus being carried to the shore on a seashell might be freely translated into English as follows:

> And born within [the white foam],
> in rare and joyous acts
> a maiden with a heavenly race
> by playful zephyrs is pushed to the shore.
> She travels on a sea-shell; and it seems
> that the heavens rejoice.[67]
>
> You might swear that the goddess
> came out of the waves
> squeezing with her right hand her hair
> and covering the sweet fruit with the other.[68]

Medici Venus, c. 1st century B.C., a type of the *Venus pudica*

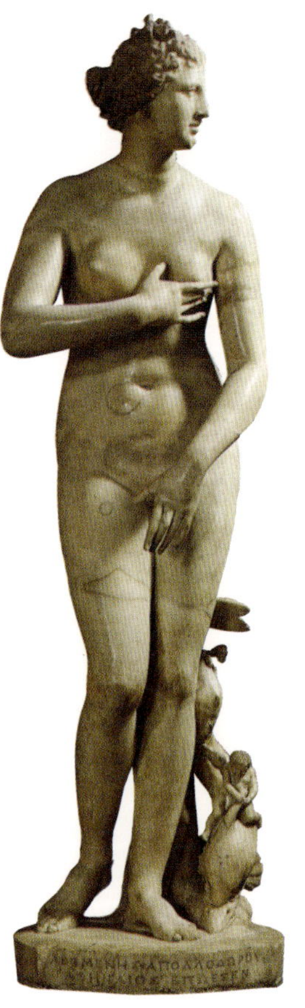

At this point the painter does stray slightly from this literary source, since Poliziano's Venus covers her breast with her left hand, whereas in Botticelli's painting it is her right hand. In Poliziano's case this difference may be explained by the fact that he did not simply rely on literary sources but also had before him a copy of a classical sculpture of the *Venus pudica*, a modest Venus covering her bosom with her right hand and her lower body with her left. An accurate description of the statue would have disturbed the meter of his stanza: the word *dextra* (right) scans better in the context than the three syllables of *sinistra* (left). Botticelli then corrects this inaccuracy in his painting and, in fact, follows the model of the *Venus pudica* very closely (see right). It is known that as early as the fourteenth century, a private collector in Florence owned classical sculptures which were attributed to the renowned Greek sculptor Polyclitus.[69] Shortly before Botticelli painted *The Birth of Venus*, Giovanni Pisano had taken the *Venus pudica* as the model for his *Temperantia* (Moderation), who is depicted on one of the columns of his marble pulpit for the cathedral of Pisa.[70] However, Botticelli did create his own version of the scene: Venus is holding a luxurious bundle of her long hair — which does not happen at all in the classical model. This addition was in keeping with Poliziano's description, whose stanza contains a reference to this motif, as do the Greek verses in the *Anthologia Greca*.

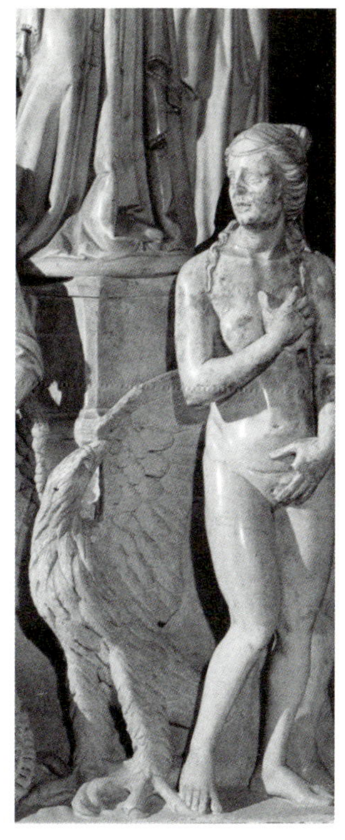

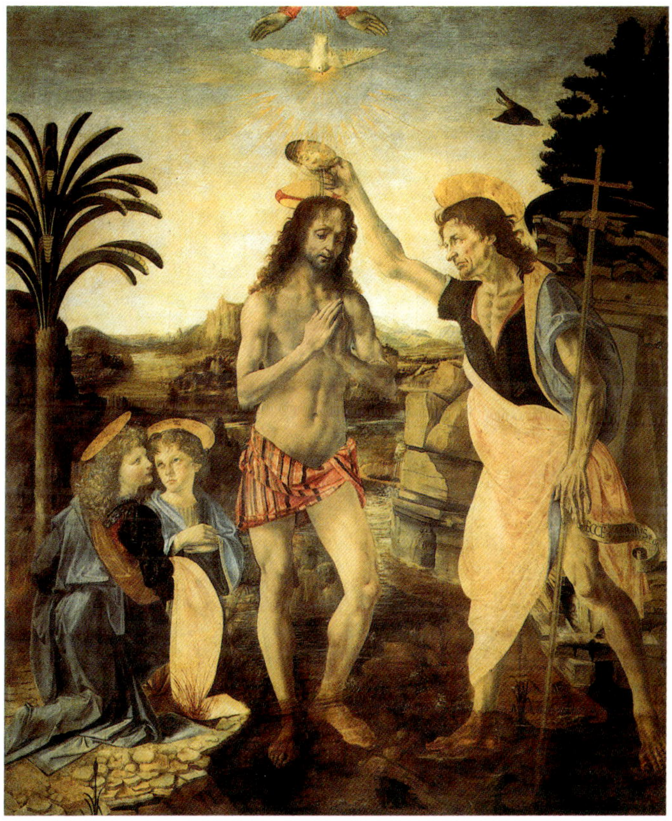

Giovanni Pisano
Temperantia (Moderation), 1302–12
Detail from marble pulpit, Cathedral of Pisa

Right: Andrea del Verrocchio and Leonardo da Vinci
The Baptism of Christ, c. 1470–75

Thus Botticelli made use of surviving artworks from antiquity, classical literary texts, as well as verses by his poetic advisor Poliziano. In the fifteenth century there was as yet no usable visual tradition portraying the

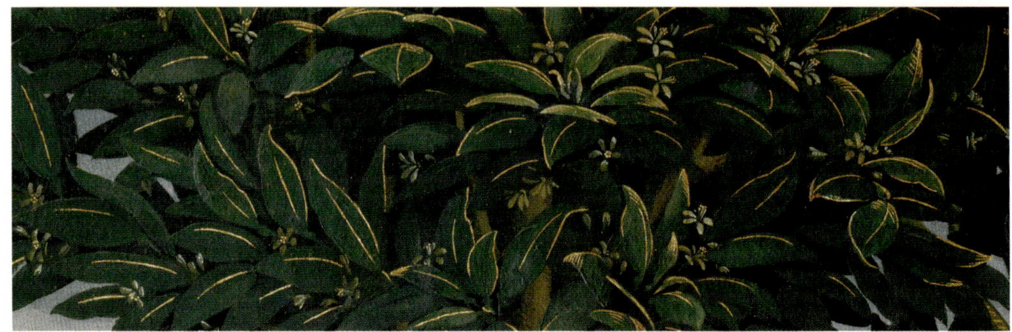

Anemone, known as the windflower since ancient times

actual arrival of Venus along with the secondary figures involved. Therefore, as before in *La Primavera,* the artist draws on a formal model that has nothing to do with the story of Venus, as far as its contents are concerned. In fact Botticelli's composition, with Venus and the Hora placed to her right, corresponds to a pictorial structure that was very commonly found in fifteenth-century Italian paintings depicting the Baptism of Christ (see p. 91). Venus in Botticelli's painting, like Christ at his baptism, remains relatively immobile in the centre of the picture space, while the Hora, stepping forward with her right arm outstretched, occupies a similar position to that of John the Baptist.[71]

It is clear from our observations thus far that both the artist and the artist's patron wanted to capture a particular moment, namely the arrival of Venus, and not her birth. Particularly noteworthy in this context are the roses which are caught in the wind on the left and strewn across the sea. They may be regarded as the roses of Venus and of love triumphant as they were described by the Greek poets, in the writings of Anacreon and others. From Hesiod's *Theogony* we learn, in addition, that Venus (Aphrodite) owed her existence to an act of cruel violence. At the behest of his mother, Saturn (Cronus) stole upon his father, Uranus, who was in the act of love and castrated him. When Saturn threw Uranus's genitals into the sea, a mighty foam billowed up all around them, and it was out of this foam that Venus, the goddess of love, was born. During this remarkable birth at sea, a rose bush grew on land as a floral equivalent to the goddess of love who had emerged from the sea at the same moment, and who would henceforth always be associated with rose plants. Apparently the rose bush, marking *The Birth of Venus*, bloomed at the very moment when the goddess of love reached the shore of the island of Cyprus.[72]

In the lower edge of the painting, Botticelli devised an additional pictorial element in the form of a rather forlorn and isolated plant — significant to the theme of arrival. Between the Hora's feet there is an anemone, which since antiquity has been known as the wind

Anemone near the Hora's feet

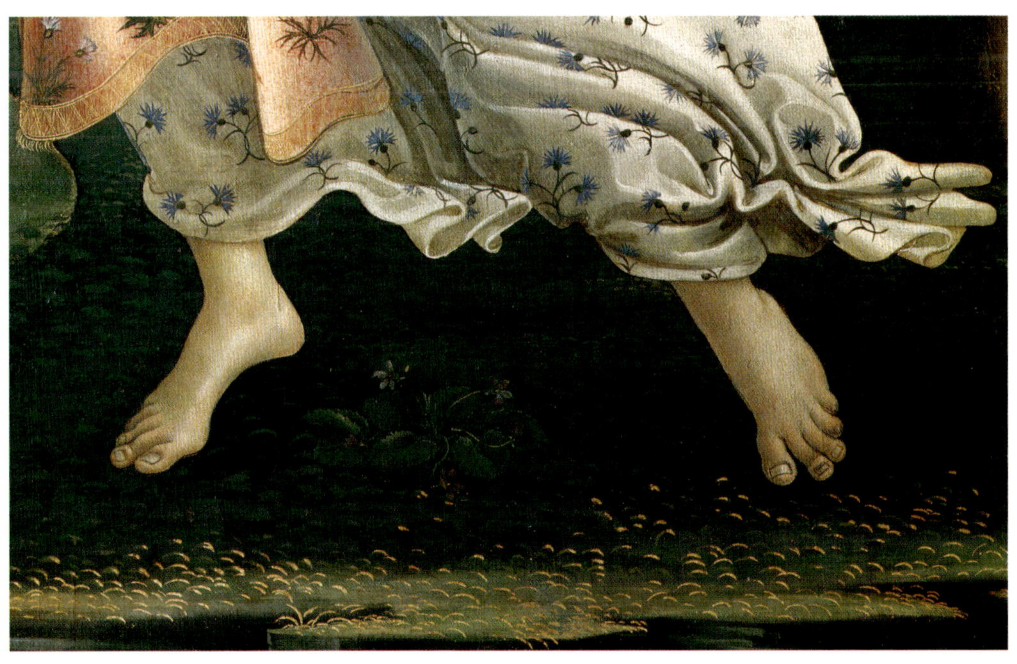

flower that blooms in the spring. According to legend, this flower only opens when the wind blows.[73] The inclusion of an anemone at the feet of the Hora is therefore wholly intentional, for there is indeed a stiff breeze coming from Zephyrus and his companion. The strong wind has brought with it the rose blossoms, which, as we have already shown, bloomed when the goddess of love reached the shore. Thus with the inclusion of an anemone, Botticelli once again underlines the fact that this is the arrival of Venus.

As before in *La Primavera,* here too Botticelli's composition is precisely calculated. The artist did not include an anemone by chance any more than he included the orange trees, or a further detail which has yet to be satisfactorily interpreted and, therefore, particularly worthy of our attention. In the lower left corner, where the sea extends to the picture edge as well as washing up against the shore, there are a number of plants, *typha latifolia* to be botanically precise (known in those days as *arundo*). In English their common name is bulrush. The rushes in the picture bear a total of four cobs, fruits, or seed pods, as botanists would say, filled with seeds of the plant which are carried away by the wind when the cobs burst open. By this means they are scattered across land and sea — hence the underlying idea of nature which, in this way, sees to the reproduction of the bulrush. It should, however, perhaps be said that this plant type actually has no place at the seashore. Bulrushes are fresh-water plants; they thrive in inland waters or, if need be, in stagnant water, but under no circumstances in the salty sea-water from which Venus was born and which surrounds her in Botticelli's painting as she approaches the shore. Some explanation is needed for this botanical displacement; especially since the otherwise

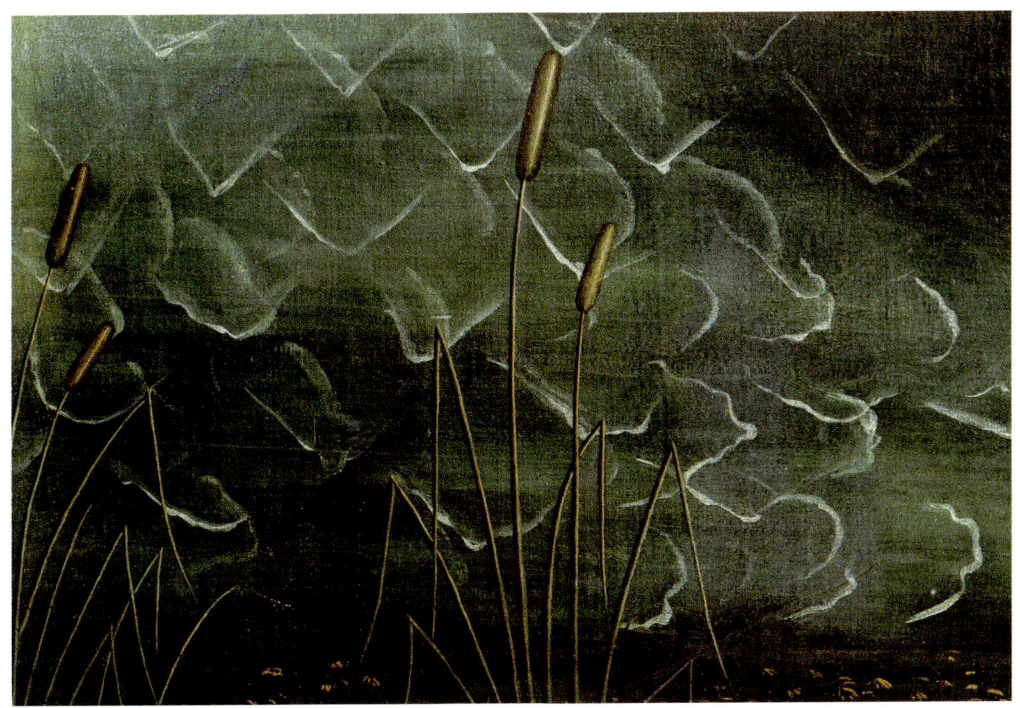

Bulrushes

meticulous detail of this mythological painting by Botticelli makes it impossible to imagine that these particular plants are included by chance alone.

Towards the end of the fifteenth century there was as yet no iconographic tradition of bulrushes in mythological paintings. *Typha latifolia* was known only from the world of Christian imagery, above all from depictions of the Baptism of Christ. Botticelli's borrowing of this general compositional type could perhaps account for the plant's inclusion in this representation of Venus. Apart from this rather superficial explanation, there are two further reasons for the inclusion of the bulrush in Botticelli's painting. At first this plant brings to mind thoughts of the circumstances of Venus's birth, which immediately preceded this scene:

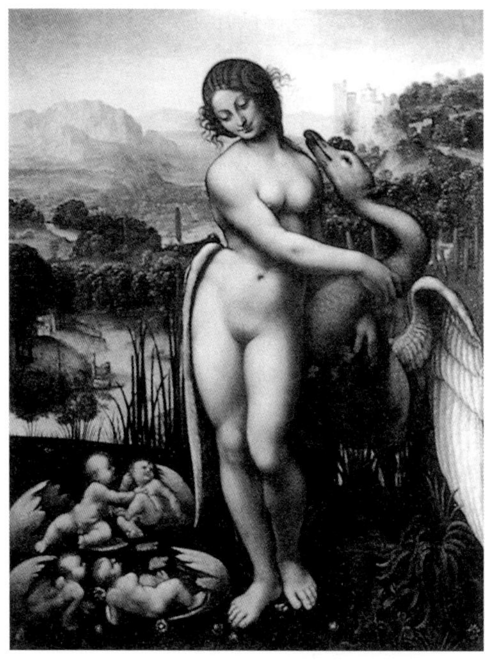

Attributed to Cesar de Sesto (School of Leonardo da Vinci) *Leda and the Swan*

In the tempestuous Aegean in the lap of Thetis
one can see the genital rod received.[74]

Poliziano does not directly describe the castrating of Uranus here, but only mentions his amputated member — *fusto genitale* — which then fell into the sea. The poet's choice of words is significant. In Italian the noun *fusto* means both the stem of a plant and a reed, while the Latin original word *fustis* means a cudgel or a stick. Thus, in his choice of words, the poet is alluding to Uranus's still erect member, and it may be assumed that Botticelli's bulrushes are an echo of this phallic allusion.

The phallic associations of the bulrush in Botticelli's painting, which were perhaps inspired by Poliziano's choice of words, are also found in other sources.[75] Besides literary confirmation of the erotic connotations of the bulrush, there is also a pictorial tradition. Thus, either in the 1490s or in the early 1500s, Leonardo da Vinci painted a picture showing the classical erotic theme of Leda and the Swan. This thematic composition is above all known from a number of other works based on it by painters of the Leonardo school, such as the oil painting in the Pembroke Collection in Salisbury, England (see p. 96). But a drawing by Leonardo himself also shows *Leda and the Swan* with bulrushes.[76] Without doubt both the painting and the drawing are of an erotic nature, for Leda is approached by the desirous god Zeus (Jupiter) in the form of a swan whose aim it is to conceive children with her. These children, Pollux and Helena, as well as Castor and Clytemnestra (according to some versions of the story)[77] represent the result of

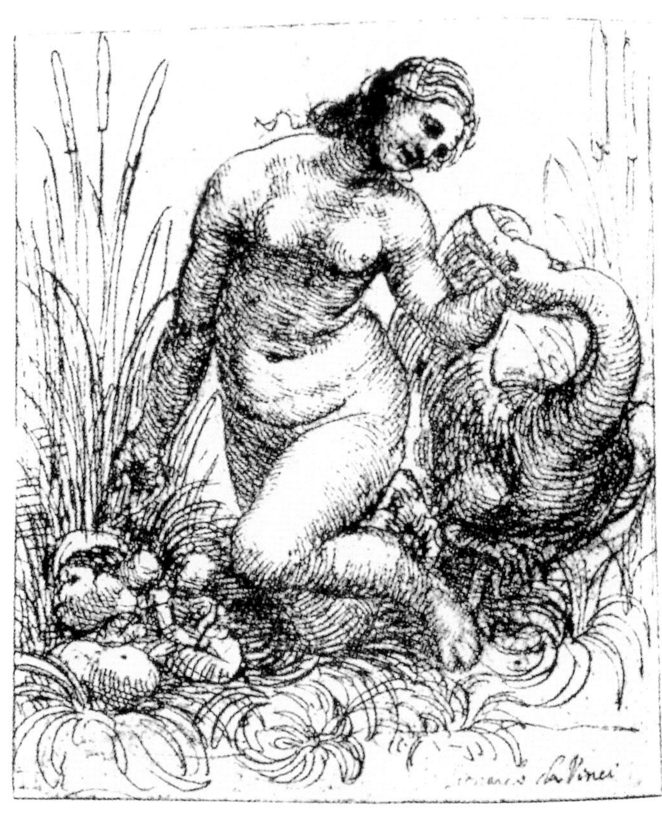

Leonardo da Vinci
Leda and the Swan

the implied sexual union between Leda and Zeus/Jupiter in the guise of a swan. Therefore, the presence of bulrushes in this drawing may well have been for erotic purposes; they are just as much an allusion to the erect male member as the encounter between Leda and the Swan is an allusion to the sexual act itself. In view of Leonardo's confirmation of the meaning of this pictorial tradition, we may presume a similar intention in Botticelli's painting of the arrival of Venus, with bulrushes again appearing as erotic symbols.

On the basis of the scarcely concealed nudity of Venus, plus the various interpretations that may be derived from the bulrushes and the shell, the so-called *Birth of Venus* may more readily be regarded as an erotic painting than *La Primavera*. Yet ultimately, without precise knowledge of the circumstances of its genesis, any interpretation must remain incomplete — the individual pictorial elements are too ambiguous. The one thing we can be certain of is that Botticelli's painting does not portray the birth of Venus, but her arrival; this is particularly evident from the winds driving her towards land, along with the anemone and the roses carried through the turbulent air. In an equally unambiguous manner, the painter includes the Hora, thus underscoring the notion of Venus being greeted upon her arrival, for the former's expansive gesture of welcome dominates the whole right side of the picture and at the same time restrains the left-to-right movement of the composition. Botticelli, his advisor and his patron clearly set considerable store by the precise depiction of the moment of arrival: the moment immediately before the goddess stepped ashore.

Most mythological panel paintings and works on canvas in fifteenth-century Florence owe their existence to some important occasion, often a wedding. The theme for Botticelli's *The Birth of Venus*, therefore, could well be connected with events in his patron's family, perhaps — as has recently been suggested — a birth.[78] In view of the erotic content of the picture it might seem more likely that it is linked with the anticipated arrival of a young woman, a bride perhaps, in the groom's house. It could be a courtship picture painted during the marriage negotiations in order to hasten the bride's agreement or that of her family. In this sense *The Birth of Venus* could equally well have been painted in conjunction with the wedding of Lorenzo di Pierfrancesco de' Medici (discussed earlier), or for a later event of this kind, namely the marriage of Piero de' Medici and Alfonsina Orsini in 1488, or in connection with the marriage of Giovanni de' Medici and Caterina Sforza in 1497. Yet all these attempts at interpreting the picture must remain purely speculative as long as there is no way to convincingly link the precise circumstances of these events with the commissioning of this picture. Whatever the case, the motif of arrival, which is repeatedly reinforced in Botticelli's painting, would have to be linked to some concrete event. Further research in this direction could be crucial in finally determining the meaning of Botticelli's *The Birth of Venus*.

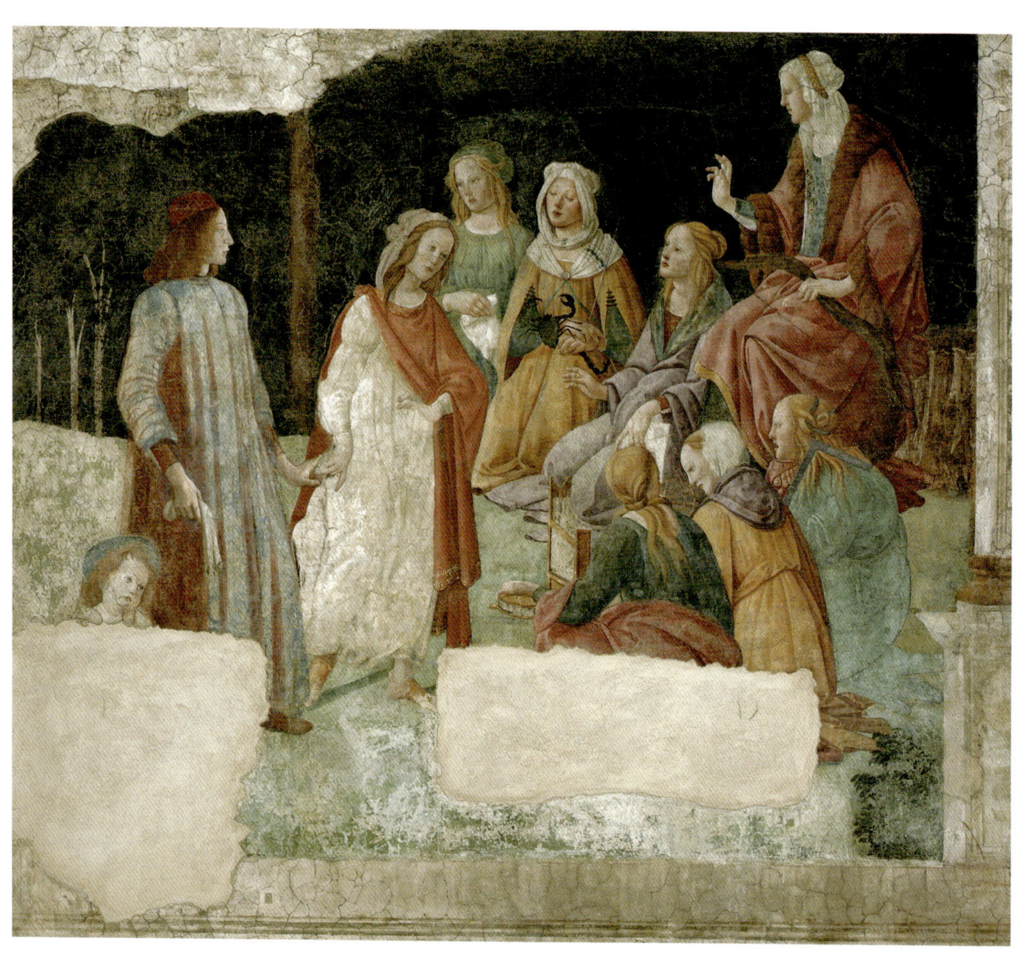

Lorenzo Tornabuoni Presented to the Liberal Arts, c. 1488

The Villa Lemmi Frescoes: Eternal Love after Death?

Three Graces, albeit in a different arrangement and with a very different meaning to those in *La Primavera,* also appear in the only profane frescoes by Sandro Botticelli which still exist. These are the Villa Lemmi frescoes, which take their name from their original location, a villa outside Florence, which in the nineteenth century belonged to a family of that name. These frescoes, which were later taken off the walls and which have only partially survived in a severely damaged state, were possibly painted in 1486 on the occasion of the marriage between Lorenzo Tornabuoni and Giovanna Albizzi.[79] There are, however, records which indicate that another series of paintings was made for this same wedding: works that depicted the story of the Jason and the Argonauts.[80] This makes a different interpretation of the frescoes' purpose seem more likely: the frescoes may well have been made following the untimely death of the bride in October 1488 to portray an ideal reunion of bride and bridegroom in the realm of immortal virtue and beauty.

Initially, leaving aside any specific interpretation, these frescoes quite clearly address a woman on the one hand and a man on the other. The scene which is didactically intended for the male viewer is played out in front of a dark background, evidently in front of a small wood, although the tree trunks can barely be distinguished now. In the foreground and middle ground the viewer sees a group of seven female figures sitting at various heights in a semi-circle and awaiting the arrival of a young man

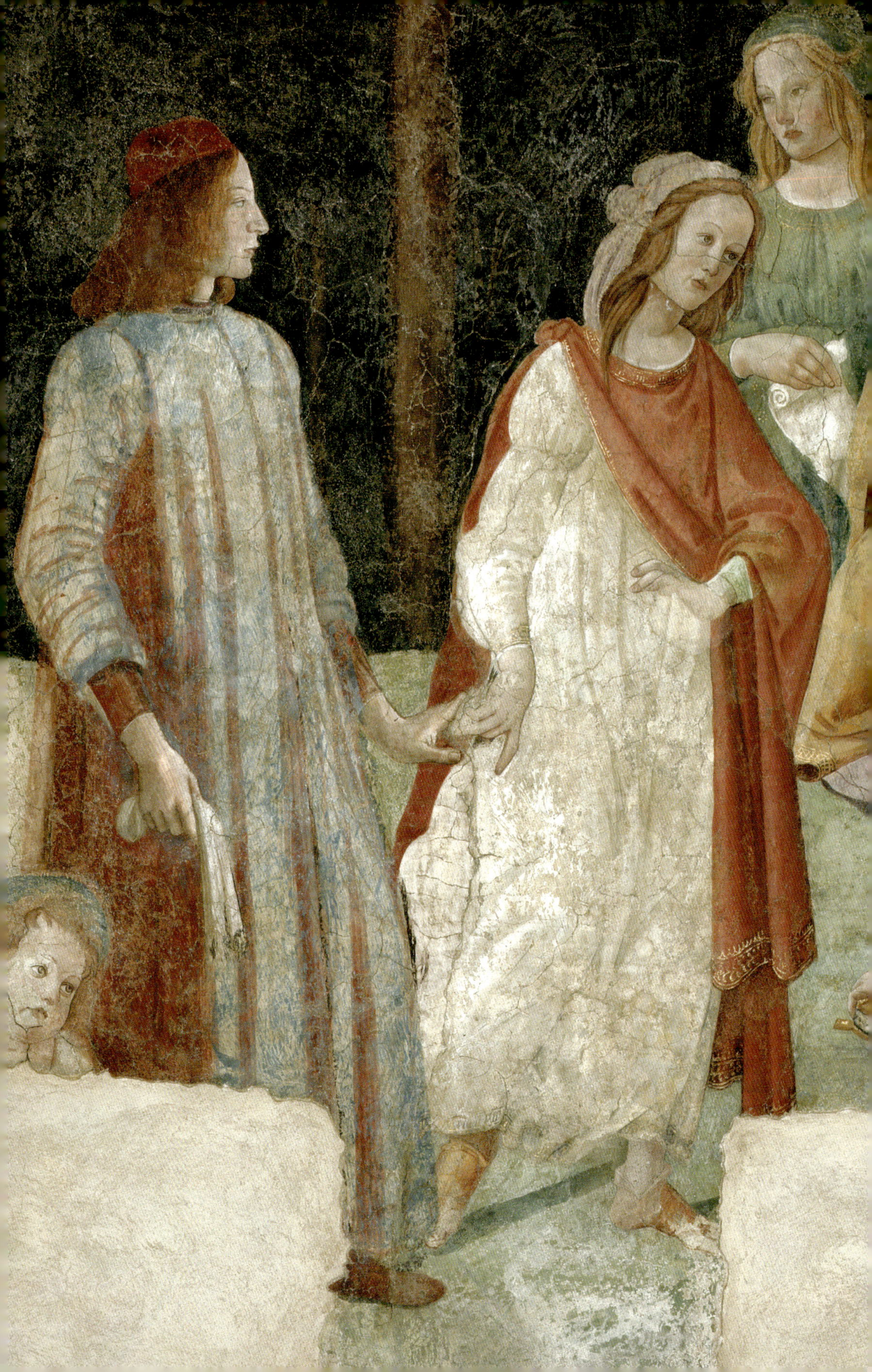

approaching from the left. This young man, Lorenzo Tornabuoni, is being led by an eighth female figure. Even further to the left it is possible to distinguish the head of a putto. On the basis of earlier descriptions, we know that the putti on the frescoes once held or brought with them shields bearing the coats of arms of the Tornabuoni and Albizzi families (in one case it is still possible to see a shield). The young women are wearing clothes reminiscent of classical images, while Lorenzo is approaching them wearing blue-coloured contemporary clothing and a red scholar's cap. In contrast to the woman next to him, he is wearing sturdy shoes, by which Botticelli characterizes him as a contemporary figure. From the portrayal of the whole scene, but above all from the attributes of the young women, it is clear that the young man is entering into the circle of the Seven Liberal Arts. In antiquity, the Seven Liberal Arts — *septem artes liberales* — constituted that branch of learning which only free citizens could pursue, for they were not open to the lower social classes, unlike the technical arts — *artes mecanicae*. In the Middle Ages the elevated *artes liberales* formed the canon of acquirable knowledge and in the fifteenth century were regarded as the yardstick of civilized behaviour.[81] They were portrayed as young women with suitable attributes and divided into two groups. The first group forming the *trivium* consisted of Grammar, Dialectic (Logic) and Rhetoric, while the second forming the *quadrivium* consisted of Arithmetic, Geometry, Astrology and Music.

Grammar leading Lorenzo Tornabuoni

In Botticelli's fresco the personification of Grammar, dressed in white and tawny red, leads the young man by his right hand into the picture space towards the circle of the other arts. In contrast to her sisters, she is not recognizable by an attribute, but by her leading role among the *artes liberales* as described by the Florentine poet Burchiello in the fifteenth century:

> Seven there are of the Liberal Arts, and first Grammar
> shows the others the way.[82]

Immediately above Grammar, we see Rhetoric dressed in green, recognizable by her attribute, the scroll. Next to her is the personification of Dialectic, who has a staff in her right hand and a frighteningly large scorpion in her left. However, the creature here is only a symbol and therefore presents no danger at all; its claws represent the opposing positions of dialectic thought. Further to the right is Arithmetic, who is identifiable by a piece of paper in her left hand with arithmetical calculations on it. In the foreground with their backs to the viewer are (from left to right) Music with her organ and tambourine, Astrology with an astrolabe, and Geometry dressed in green and carrying a T-square on her shoulder. Above the circle of the Seven Liberal Arts is a proportionally larger, more grandly dressed female figure. In her left hand she carries a bow and her right hand is raised in a gesture of greeting, which is reminiscent of period book illustrations (see p. 66) and the figure of Venus in Botticelli's *La Primavera.* This female figure is most probably Phronesis, the mother of Philology. Whatever the case, she is clearly in some way superior to the Liberal Arts. It is therefore clear that Grammar is not only leading the young man into the realm of the *septem artes liberales* but is also presenting him to Phronesis. Thus, in accordance with the traditions of antiquity and in keeping with the canon of the medieval universities, he is credited with exceptional prowess in all the branches of acquirable knowledge. Moreover, one may presume that the *quadrivium*

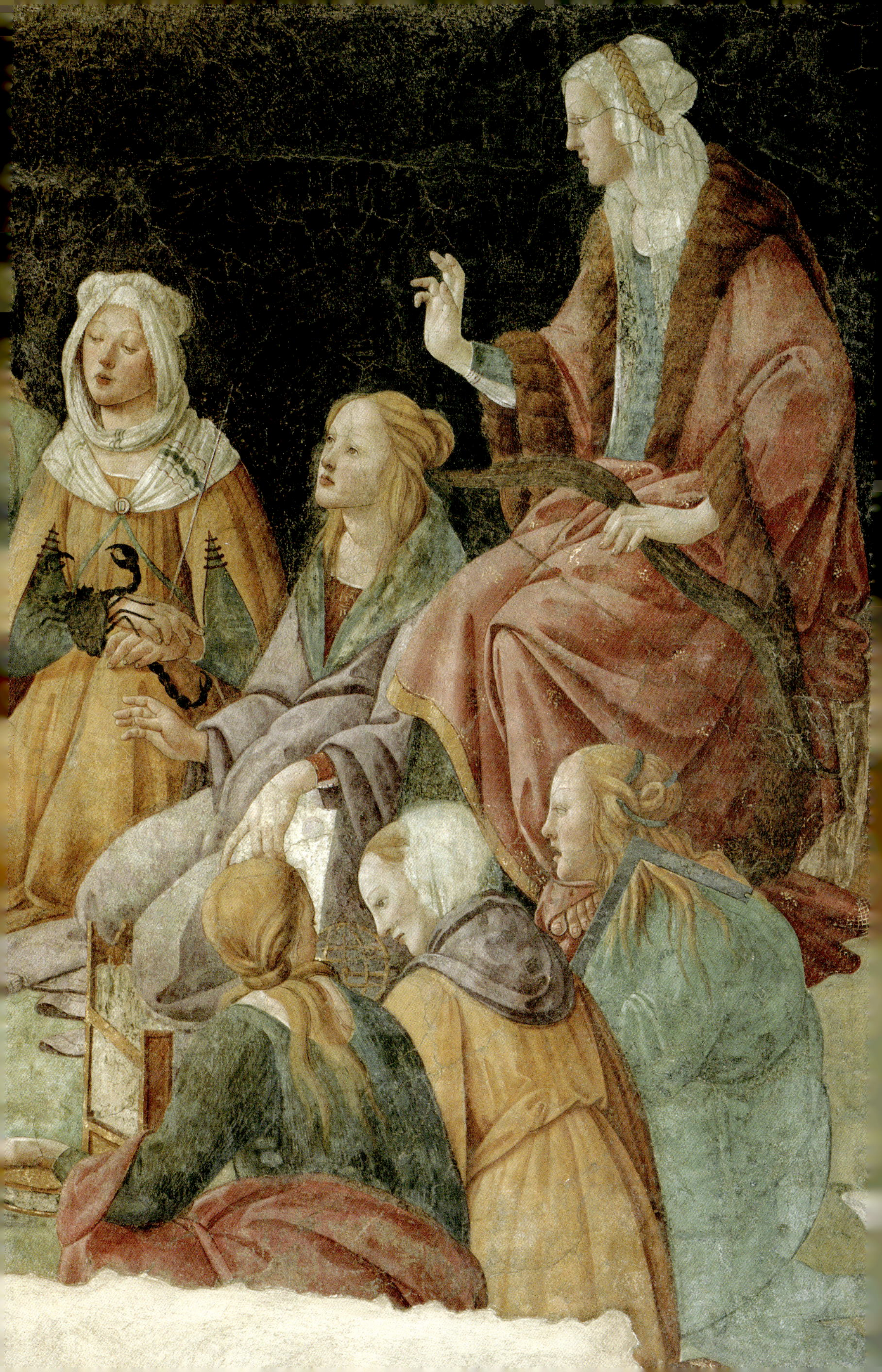

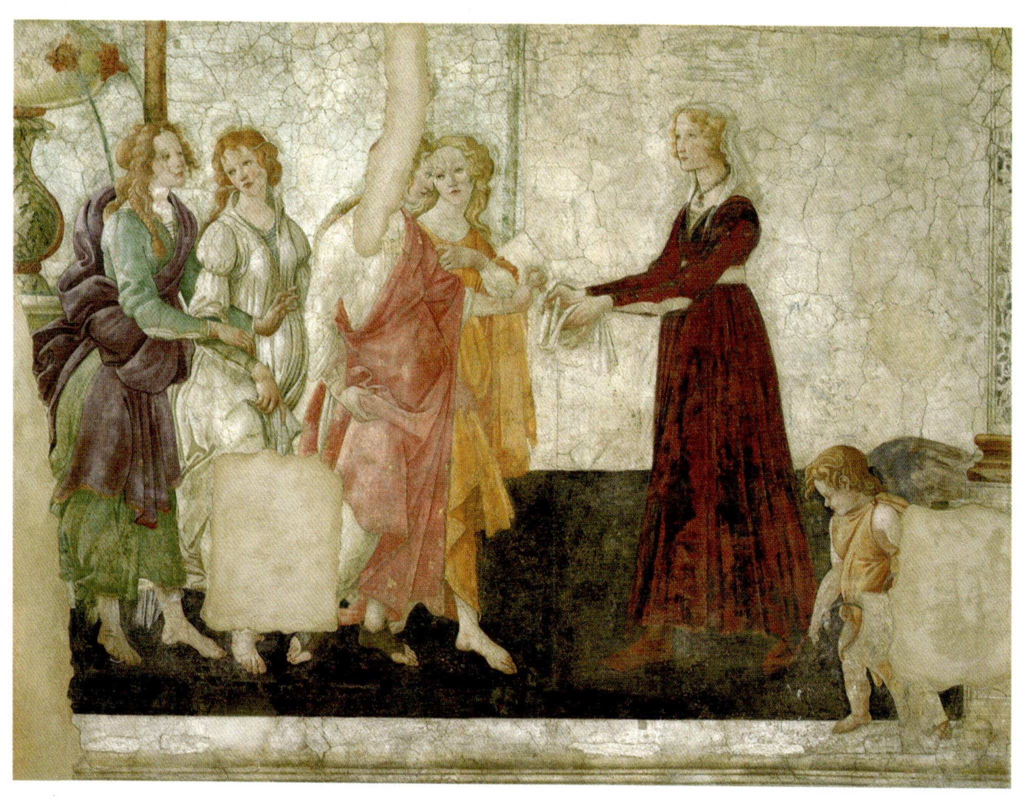

Giovanna Albizzi, Venus and the Three Graces, c. 1488

was not so close to his heart as the *trivium*, for the personifications of Grammar, Dialectic, and Rhetoric are portrayed *en face* while Geometry, Astrology, and Music are seen from behind and thus seem less important.

In direct contrast to the portrayal of the Seven Liberal Arts, and their implied meaning for the young man's level of education, is the second fresco, which seems more directed towards a female role, with the Three Graces and Venus on the left and Giovanna Albizzi on the right. In this case the scene is set in front of a much lighter background, probably in a walled garden, to judge by the glimpse of a well on the left and the white walls visible in the background. The placement of the figures in a comparatively enclosed-looking space contrasts with the much more open aspect of the first fresco which focuses on the male role. This contrast is clearly to be understood as a pointer towards the gender-specific division of roles. The world beyond the home was regarded as the husband's domain, while his wife was confined to the realms of domesticity, including the garden; the husband operates in the sciences and the arts, his wife in the sphere of beauty and grace.

The spatial division of this garden, which echoes the *hortus conclusus* of the Virgin Mary, is clearer and stricter than in the first fresco. On the right we see Giovanna Albizzi wearing a contemporary brown dress with a white sash. The almost vertical folds of the material have a certain static quality. Her brown shoes, like her dress, are barely perceptible against the similarly coloured ground. Her hair is largely covered by a loose white scarf, and in her outstretched hands she is holding a similar white cloth which forms a link to the group in the left half of the picture. The Three Graces and Venus are entering the picture space from that side; light-footed

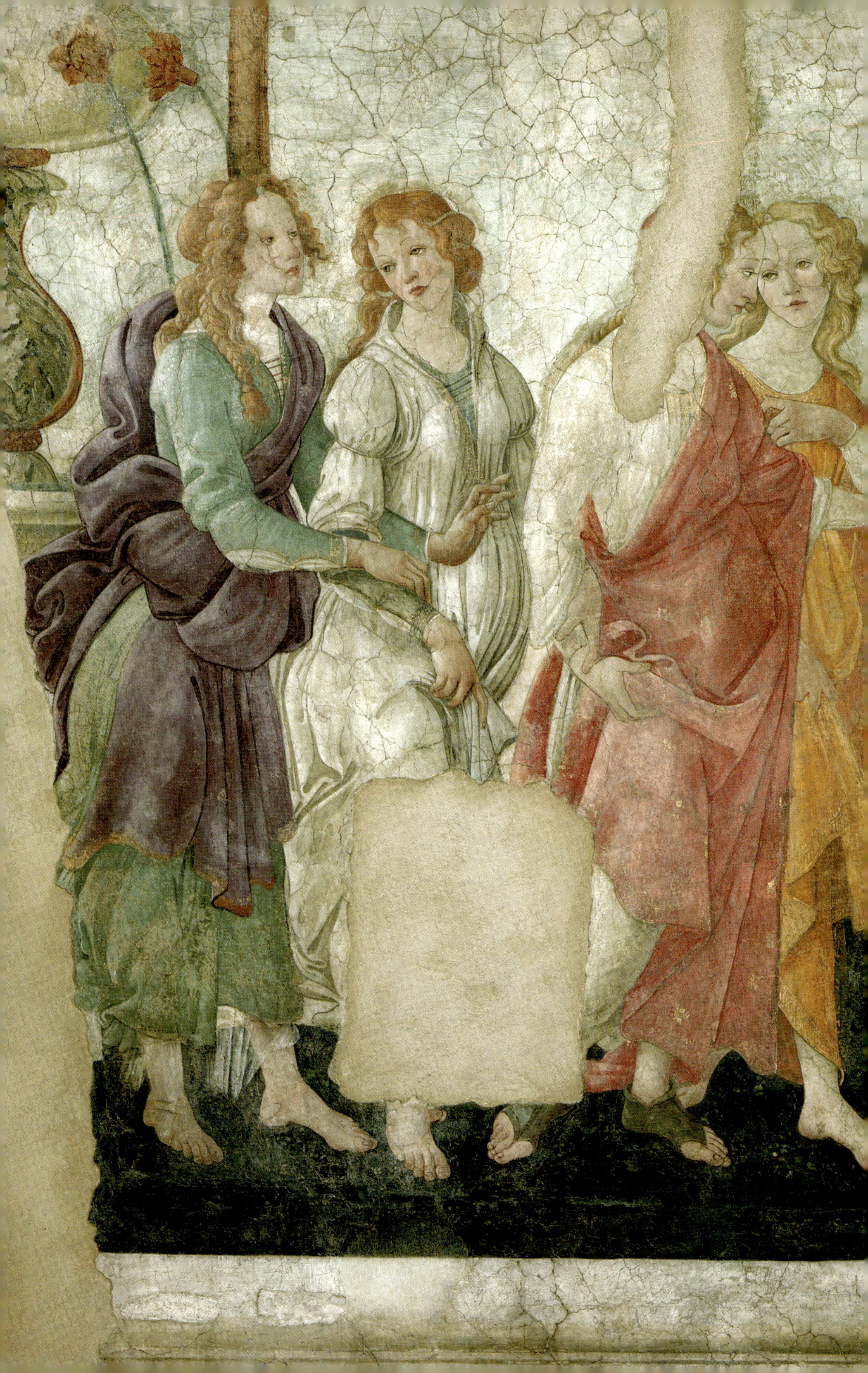

and dressed in flowing, billowing gowns, they approach the centre of the picture. They present a marked contrast to the figure of Giovanna waiting on the right. Their loose, more colourful gowns clearly reveal a certain degree of movement. Three of the young women are barefoot, while the fourth who leads the group and is therefore also the most important, wears sandals of a type that might have been worn in antiquity. At least two of the women, whose faces the viewer can see, are extremely similar to each other. Even more than in the scene with the Liberal Arts, here there is a clear contrast between the contemporary clothing of the isolated figure on the right and the classical-style gowns of the group on the left. This group consists of allegorical figures who are further distinguished from each other by the sandals of the young woman in front, for they signify her as Venus, the goddess, with the Three Graces. Incidentally, this same distinction is made in Botticelli's *La Primavera,* where only Venus and Mercury have shoes, while the Graces have none.

As in his other works, Botticelli combines a variety of literary and artistic sources to produce the Tornabuoni Villa frescoes. Thus, in some respects, the attributes of the Liberal Arts are in keeping with descriptions of medieval accounts, and in other respects with corresponding depictions in the Spanish Chapel of Santa Maria Novella in Florence.[83] There, in Andrea di Bonaiuto's *Triumph of St. Thomas Aquinas* (1366–68), Botticelli found a comprehensive grouping of the medieval system of the sciences and the arts. However, for Botticelli's portrayal of the Liberal Arts and their relationship to Lorenzo Tornabuoni, these propagandistic, Dominican images were certainly less influential than Martianus Capella's *De nuptiis Philologiae et Mercurii.* In the first two of

Venus and the Three Graces

his allegorical-mythological books the author describes the marriage between the god Mercury and his mortal bride, Philology, who is made immortal specifically for this wedding. Though Martianus Capella writes about a wedding, in a deeper sense the subject is the elevation of Philology to immortality. And it is precisely this notion of immortality woven into the allegorical framework of a wedding between Philology and Mercury which may well be at the root of Botticelli's fresco. In that case Mercury, in the text by Martianus Capella, could be regarded as the mythological counterpart to Lorenzo Tornabuoni, who enters into the realm of Phronesis, the mother of Philology — the realm of the sciences and the arts — and thus secures access to a world of immortal values.

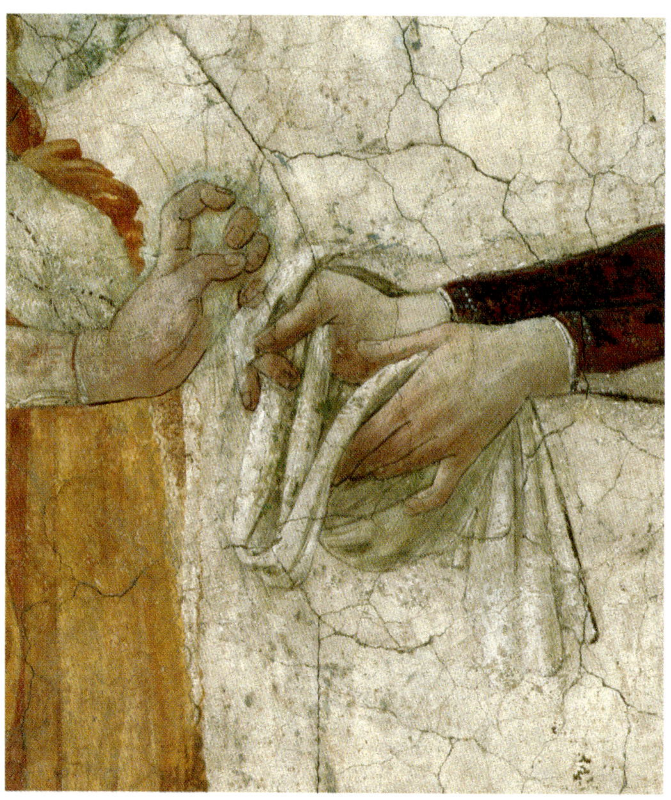

Giovanna Albizzi's hands

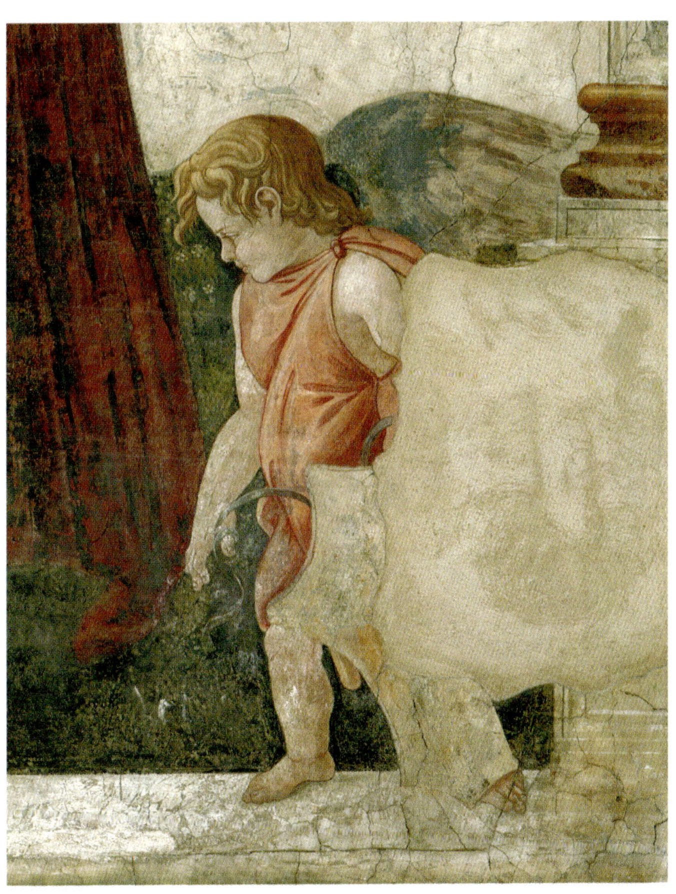

Putto with Albizzi family coat of arms

The second fresco presents a sequence related to that of the first. According to Martianus Capella, Philology is rewarded for her beauty and virtue with immortality, and the young departed Giovanna, the "alter ego" of Philology takes the same path. She has attained the realm of Venus and the Graces — the realm of eternal beauty, grace, and virtue, qualities symbolized by Venus and the Three Graces.[84] This re-interpretation of a wedding allegory in light of the death of Giovanna would be entirely in keeping with the desire of the cultured Lorenzo Tornabuoni, both to give expression to his grief over the loss of his wife, and to be close to his late wife in an imaginary, timeless realm of the arts and the virtues. The strangely dressed putti, whose primary function in both paintings is to bear the families' coats of arms, in fact embody that grief. They are certainly far removed from customary notions of lively little fellows who frequently can barely disguise their kinship with bold Armor. The putto in the first fresco with Lorenzo gazes sadly and dreamily out of the picture without focusing on anything in particular. His counterpart in the second fresco approaches with his head bowed and carries the coat of arms of Giovanna's family, just as though it had lost its most treasured possession. He too is lost in silent grief, which alone serves as a reminder that death can never be banished from the world, neither by love nor by beauty. Yet, at the same time, the two frescoes also show that death may be overcome and that, after his wife's untimely death, the widower may be united with her in a realm of mythological transfiguration. Lorenzo reaches his lost, distant loved-one both through his love and through his own closeness to immortality, which he achieves with the help of the sciences and the arts. As a consequence of her beauty, grace and virtue on this earth, Giovanna is already part of this realm of eternity and immortality. If this interpretation is valid, these frescoes are the most impressive examples of painting in which — to recall the ideas of Marsilio Ficino as quoted at the beginning of this book — the beauty of the image demonstrates virtue to the viewer, and here even brings the lovers together beyond death. Perhaps more than any other of Botticelli's mythological works, these two paintings for Lorenzo demonstrate the deeply affecting power of images as well as the strength of love itself.

Literary Appendix on *La Primavera*

1. Virgil, *The Aeneid*, 4.242–246, Translated into English with an introduction by W. F. Jackson Knight, London, 1st edition 1956, p. 104:
"Then he took his wand; the wand with which he calls the pale souls forth from the Nether World and sends others down to grim Tartarus, gives sleep, and takes sleep away, and unseals eyes at death. So shepherding the winds before him with his wand, he swam through the murk of the clouds."

2. Seneca, "On Benefits," 1.3.2–7, in: *Moral Essays*, with an English translation by John W. Basore, London and Cambridge, Mass. 1935, vol. 3, pp. 13 and 15:
"Of the nature and property of these [benefits] I shall speak later if you will permit me first to digress upon questions that are foreign to the subject — why the Graces are three in number and why they are sisters, why they have their hands interlocked, and why they are smiling and youthful and virginal and are clad in loose and transparent garb. Some would have it appear that there is one for bestowing a benefit, another for receiving it, and a third for returning it; others hold that there are three classes of benefactors — those who earn benefits, those who return them, those who receive and return them at the same time. But of the two explanations do you accept as true whichever you like; yet what profit is there in such knowledge? Why do the sisters hand in hand dance in a ring which returns upon itself? For the reason that a benefit passing in its course from hand to hand returns nevertheless to the giver; the beauty of the whole is destroyed if the course is anywhere broken, and it has the most beauty if it is continuous and maintains an uninterrupted succession. In the dance, nevertheless, an older sister has especial honour, as do those who earn benefits. Their faces are cheerful, as are ordinarily the faces of those who bestow or receive benefits. They are young because the memory of benefits ought not to grow old. They are maidens because benefits are pure and undefiled and holy in the eyes of all; and it is fitting that there should be nothing to bind or restrict them, and so the maidens wear flowing robes, and these, too, are transparent because benefits desire to be seen.... And the reason that Mercury stands with them is, not that argument or eloquence commends benefits, but simply that the painter chose to picture them so."

3. Leon Battista Alberti, *On Painting and On Sculpture: The Latin Texts of De Pictura and De Statua*, edited with translations, introductions, and notes by Cecil Grayson, London 1972, 2.45 and 3.54, pp. 87,97:
"The movements of hair and manes and branches and leaves and clothing are very pleasing when represented in painting. I should like all the seven movements I spoke of to appear in hair. Let it twist around as if to tie itself in a knot, and wave upwards in the air like flames, let it weave beneath other hair and sometimes lift on one side and another. The bends and curves of branches should be partly arched upwards, partly directed downwards; some should stick out towards you, others recede, and some should be twisted like ropes. Similarly in the folds of garments care should be taken that, just as the branches of a tree emanate in all directions from the trunk, so folds should issue from a fold like branches. In these too all the movements should be done in such a way that in no garment is there any part in which similar movements are not to be found. But as I frequently advise, let all the movements be restrained and gentle, and represent grace rather than remarkable effort. Since by nature clothes are heavy and do not make curves at all, as they tend always to fall straight down to the ground, it will be a good idea, when we wish clothing to have some movement, to have in the corner of the picture the face of the West [Zephyrus] or South Wind blowing between the clouds and moving all the clothing before it. The pleasing result will be that those sides of the bodies the wind strikes will appear under the covering of the clothes almost as if they were naked, since the clothes are made to adhere to the body by the force of the wind; on the other sides the clothing blown about by the wind will wave appropriately up in the air."

"What shall we say too about those three young sisters, whom Hesiod called Egle, Euphronesis and Thalia? The ancients represented them dressed in loose transparent robes, with smiling faces and hands intertwined; they thereby wished to signify liberality, for one of the sisters gives, another receives and the third returns the favour, all of which degrees should be present in every act of perfect liberality."

4. Horace Ode no 1.30 in: *Carpe diem: Horace Odes I,* edited, translated, and with an introduction by David West, New York 1995, p. 143:
"Venus, queen of Cnidos and Paphos,
abandon your beloved Cyprus and move
to the lovely shrine of Glycera, who summons you
with clouds of incense.
Your ardent boy must hurry along with you
and Nymphs and Graces with their girdles loose
and Youth, so uncongenial without you,
and Mercury."

5. Titus Lucretius Carus, *De rerum natura,* 5.737–740, 1.18–23. English translation: Lucretius *De Rerum Natura* by W. H. D. Rouse, London and Cambridge, Mass. 1953, p. 393 and pp. 3 and 5:
"On come Spring and Venus, and Venus's winged harbinger marching before, with Zephyr and mother Flora a pace behind him strewing the whole path in front with brilliant colours and filling it with scents."

"... and the leafy dwellings of birds and verdant plains, striking soft love into the breasts of all creatures, thou dost cause them greedily to beget their generations after their kind. Since therefore thou alone dost govern the nature of things, since without thee nothing comes forth into the shining borders of light, nothing joyous and lovely is made..."

6. Ovid, *Fasti,* 5.193–214 on May 2 in: *Publii Ovidii Nasonis Fastorum Libri Sex,* edited with a translation and commentary by Sir James George Frazer, vol. I, pp. 261–263:
"So I spoke, and the goddess answered my question thus, and while she spoke, her lips breathed vernal roses: 'I who now am called Flora was formerly Chloris: a Greek letter of my name is corrupted in the Latin speech. Chloris I was, a nymph of the happy fields where, as you have heard, dwelt the fortunate men of old. Modesty shrinks from describing my figure; but it procured the hand of a god for my mother's daughter. Twas spring, and I was roaming; Zephyr caught sight of me; I retired; he pursued and I fled; but he was stronger.... However, he made amends for his violence by giving me the name of bride, and in my marriage-bed I have naught to complain of. I enjoy perpetual spring; most buxom is the year ever; ever the tree is clothed with leaves, the ground with pasture. In the fields that are my dower, I have a fruitful garden, fanned by the breeze and watered by a spring of running water. This garden my husband filled with noble flowers and said, "Goddess, be queen of flowers." Oft did I wish to count the colours in the beds, but could not; the number was past counting'."

Biography of the Artist

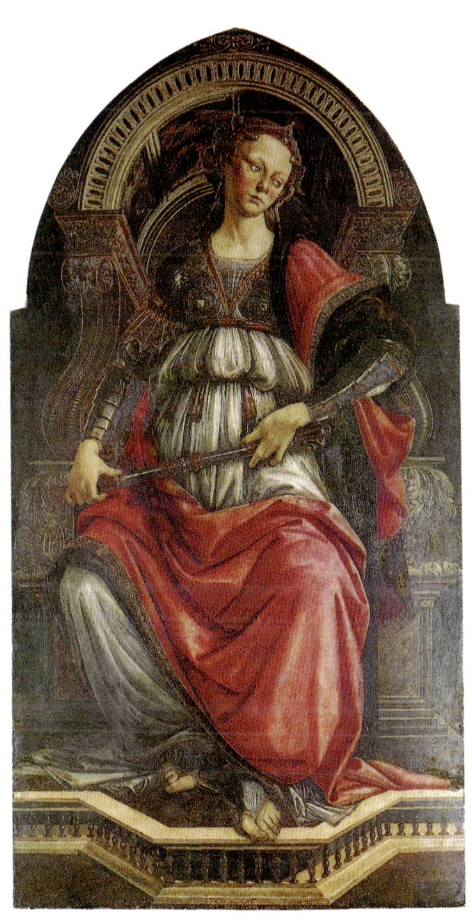

La Fortezza (Fortitude), c. 1470

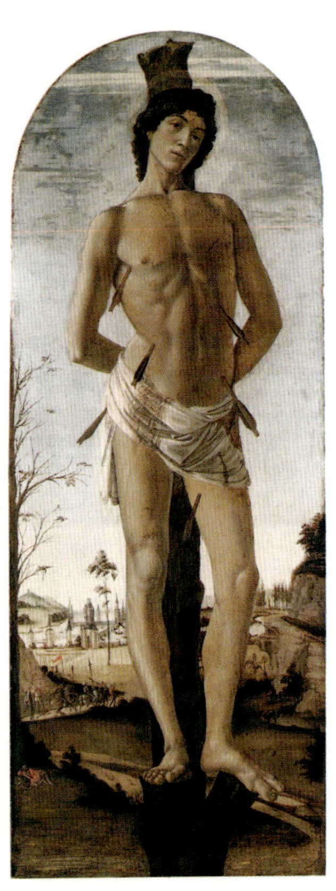

1444/1445 – 1462

Alessandro di Mariano di Vanni Filipepi, known as Sandro Botticelli, is born in Florence in 1444 or 1445 as the youngest son of Mariano Filipepi, who earned his living as a tanner. Botticelli begins his career as an artist like many other painters of his time: at the age of thirteen or fourteen, after a short period at school, he starts work as an apprentice craftsman. During his youth — if we are to believe a remark written by his father on an income-tax return — Botticelli was rather sickly. In his biography of the artist, the sixteenth-century writer Giorgio Vasari remarks that the young Sandro had little interest in reading, writing and arithmetic — the mainstays of schooling. In 1459, after his schooling, Botticelli begins his goldsmith apprenticeship — training which required neither particular mathematical talent nor an especially robust constitution. According to various accounts he took his name from the goldsmith Botticelli — although it could equally well be that the name derived from an activity in the goldsmith's workshop, namely the beating or hammering of gold or silver, which was referred to as *battiloro* or *battigello*.

In the goldsmiths workshop Botticelli also learns the basics of drawing and at the same time discovers his love of painting, which then prompts him to change direction in his professional life. In 1461 or possibly 1462, he transfers to the workshop of Filippo Lippi, the most important painter in Florence at the time. There he carries out minor commissions, such as small-scale paintings of the Madonna, which were produced in great number in the Filippo Lippi workshop. Through his teacher, but no doubt also through other contacts as well, Botticelli must have become acquainted with those leaders of Florentine society who regularly commissioned artworks. These included the Vespucci and the

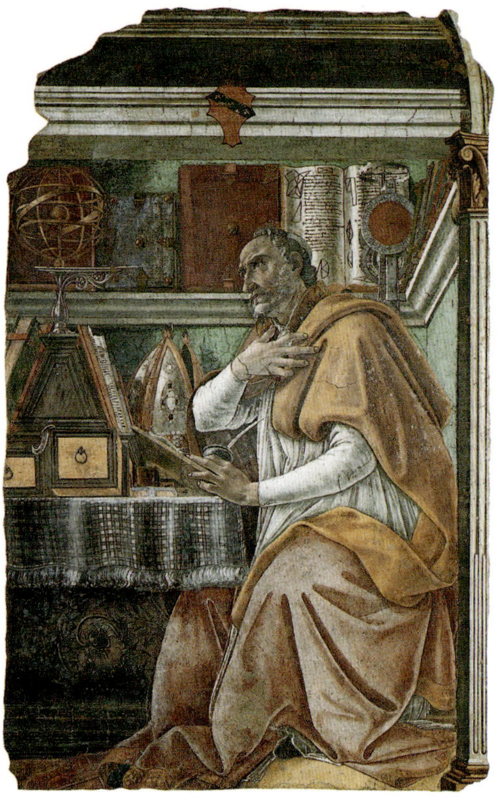

Above:
St. Sebastian,
c. 1473

Right:
St. Augustine,
1480

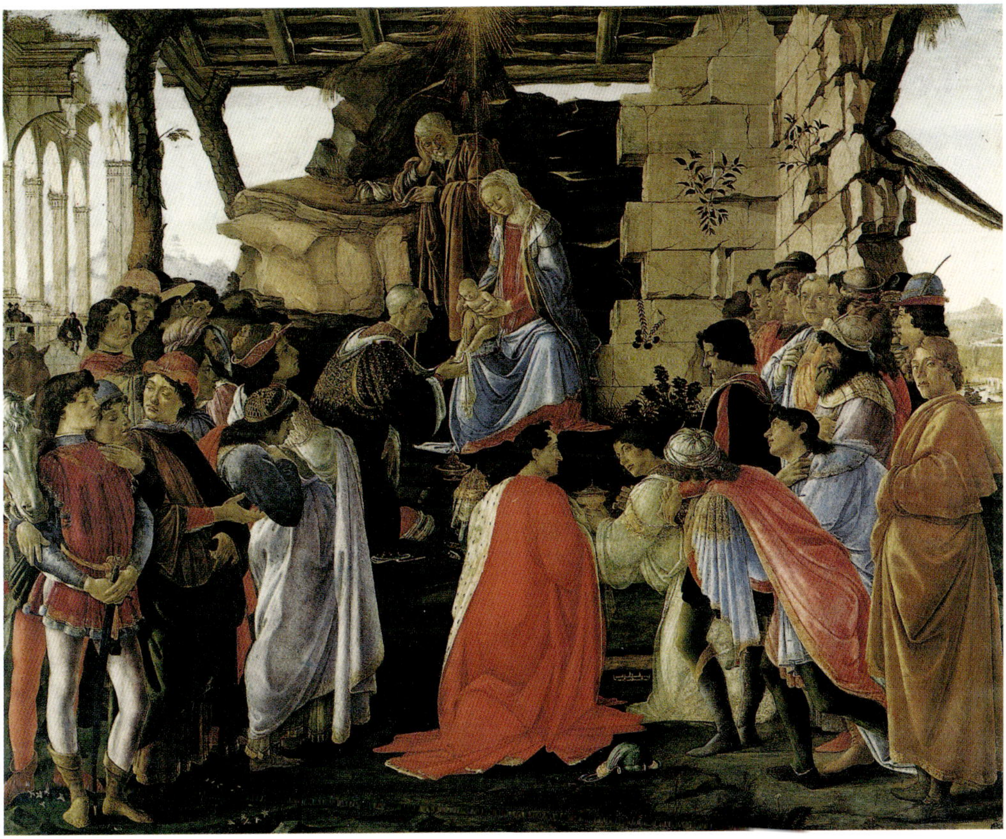

Medici, the most important families in the city at that time, who over the years commissioned the majority of Botticelli's mythological paintings.

1470–1473

From 1470 onwards Botticelli runs his own studio in his father's house, where Filippino Lippi, the son of his teacher, was also later to work. In June 1470 he receives his earliest known major commission: two panel paintings representing the Virtues for the meeting hall of the governing guild authority in Florence. Only one of these panels was completed, namely *Fortezza* (Fortitude), which can be seen today in the Uffizi Gallery. In 1472 he becomes a member of the Compagnia di San Luca, a lay brotherhood of painters. In circa 1473 he completes his *St. Sebastian* panel for the Florentine church Santa Maria Maggiore, which is now located in the Gemäldegalerie Berlin.

1474

Botticelli's first commission outside of Florence takes him to the nearby town of Pisa, where he is to paint a number of frescoes for the Camposanto, one of the oldest and most important cemeteries in central Italy. Instead of carrying out the frescoes,

Adoration of the Magi,
c. 1475–76

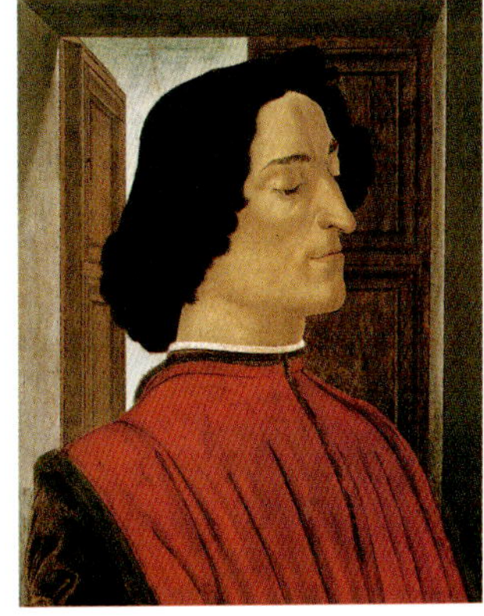

Portrait of Giuliano de' Medici,
1476–78

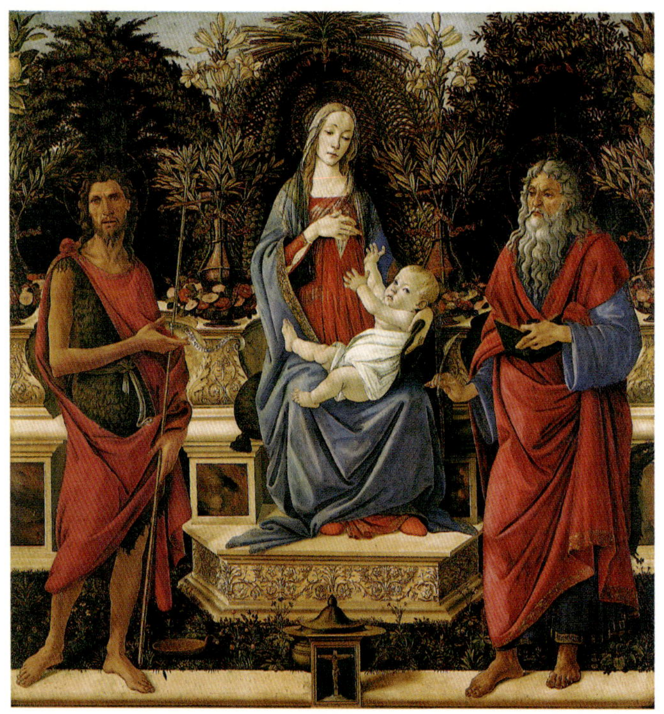

Madonna and Child with SS. John the Baptist and John the Evangelist (Bardi Altarpiece), 1484–85

however, he completes an altarpiece showing the Assumption of the Virgin; this work was destroyed in the sixteenth century. In Pisa, Botticelli has ample opportunity to see numerous sarcophagi from antiquity that were preserved there, and to study their figurative decorations. He also studies important examples of fourteenth-century Italian frescoes.

1475–1476

Botticelli produces a standard to commemorate a knightly tournament — the famous *giostra* (joust) won by Giuliano de' Medici — with a depiction of Minerva and the symbols of the Medici family (this work is no longer extant). It is possible that this standard marked the beginning of Botticelli's long involvement with the Medici.

Between 1475 and 1476 he paints *Adoration of the Magi* for the Guasparre del Lama Chapel in Santa Maria Novella in Florence. This small-format painting is well known for its inclusion of several portraits of the Medici family; it is also thought to include a self-portrait of the artist, who is on the far right, gazing towards the viewer.

1478

During the Pazzi Conspiracy against the rule of the Medici in Florence, Giuliano de' Medici, the brother of Lorenzo il Magnifico de' Medici (Lorenzo the Magnificent), is murdered. Botticelli is commissioned to depict the hanged ring-leaders at the Porta della Dogana, portraying their shame (these paintings were destroyed in 1494 when the Medici were driven out of Florence). Botticelli makes a panel portrait of the murdered Giuliano, of which a number of copies and variations are still extant.

1480

Botticelli carries out a commission for the Vespucci family to paint a fresco of St. Augustine for the church Ognissanti (All Saints) in Florence.

1481–1482

Botticelli, by now one of the most distinguished painters in Italy, is invited to Rome by Pope

Sixtus IV, where he receives the most important commission of his career: a fresco for the Sistine Chapel in the Vatican, the ceiling which Michelangelo was later to decorate. On two side walls Botticelli paints two monumental scenes from the story of Moses, a scene from the life of Christ and a number of full-length papal portraits.

It seems probable that before departing for Rome, Botticelli was commissioned to paint *La Primavera* and *Minerva and the Centaur* for the bridal chamber of Lorenzo di Pierfrancesco de' Medici and Semiramide Appiani. He completed these upon his return to Florence in the summer of 1482.

1483

For the wedding between Giannozzo Pucci and Lucrezia Bini (arranged by Lorenzo the Magnificent), Botticelli together with assistants paints four panels depicting episodes in the story of Nastagio degli Onesti from Giovanni Boccaccio's *Decamerone* — particularly dramatic portrayals of the "right" and the "wrong" way for a young woman to behave when a suitor courts her.

1485 – 1490

During this period Botticelli paints a number of important, large-scale altarpieces for patrons in Florence, including a *sacra conversazione* in 1485 for Giovanni Bardi, and a similar panel for the Guild of Physicians and Apothecaries (Medici e degli Speciali) between 1488 and 1490, a monumental Coronation of Mary for the chapel of the Goldsmiths' Guild (Orafi) in the church of San Marco. In 1490, together with Filippino Lippi, Perugino, and Domenico Ghirlandaio, he carries out various frescoes for a country residence belonging to Lorenzo the Magnificent, which are no longer extant. Around 1488 he paints the frescoes for Lorenzo Tornabuoni's villa.

1490 – 1495

Notable among the works which Botticelli completes in the early

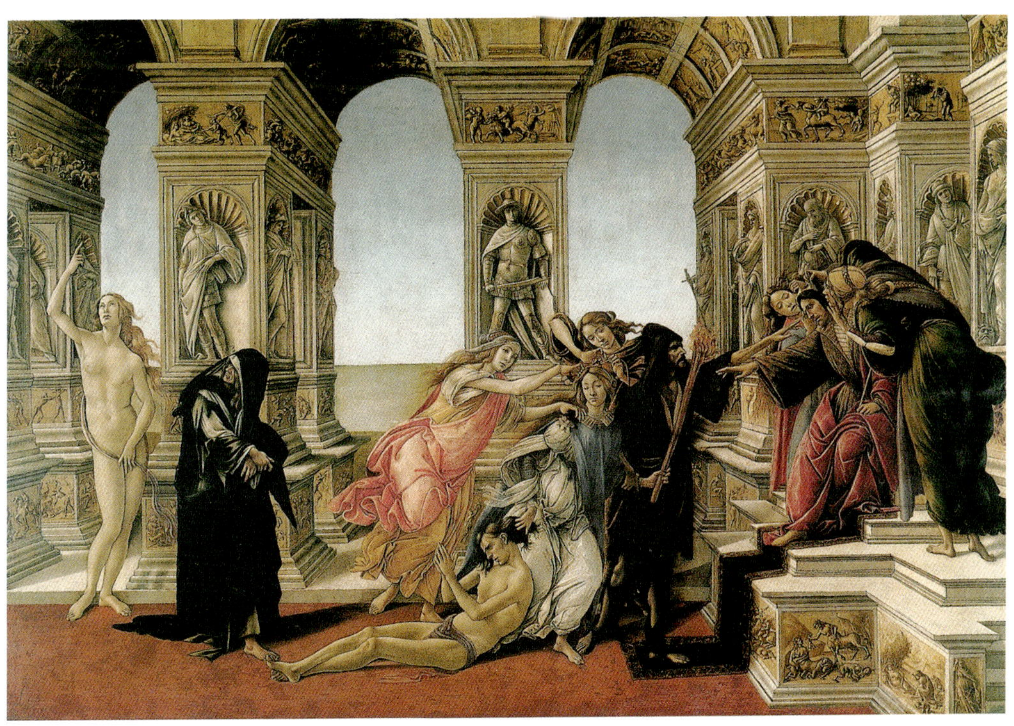

La Calunnia (*The Calumny of Apelles*), c. 1494–95

1490s are two altarpieces — pietàs that are on view today in Munich and Milan — and *La Calunnia* (*The Calumny of Apelles*), which is located today in the Uffizi Gallery. In the 1490s and in the early 1500s, Botticelli produces markedly fewer paintings than in the previous decade. Vasari suggests that the cause might have been Botticelli's involvement in the ambitious project to illustrate Dante's *Divine Comedy* for Lorenzo di Pierfrancesco de' Medici. But there may also have been other constraints on his activities as a painter: on 8 April 1492 Lorenzo the Magnificent dies. He had been one of Botticelli's most important patrons, and two years later his branch of the Medici family was driven out of Florence. At the same time, Botticelli falls increasingly under the influence of Girolamo Savonarola, the ascetic preacher who became prior of San Marco, the Florentine Dominican convent, in 1491. Among other things, Savonarola denounced corruption within the Church, and in 1497 be set up a "pyre for earthly vanities" on which luxury goods were to be burned, including non-religious paintings. However, Savonarola's political and religious zeal were soon viewed as excessive, and ultimately he was condemned as a heretic and publicly burnt at the stake in 1498.

1500 – 1510

Still affected by the sermons of Savonarola and his dramatic death, in 1501 (according to the Florentine calendar in 1500) Botticelli paints *The Mystic Nativity*, an enigmatic work which seems to reflect the deep religious experiences the painter had been through. Shortly thereafter, he paints several *spalliera* pictures: two of the stories of Virginia and Lucretia, and a series of four panels which depict scenes from the life of Saint Zenobius. In May 1510 the artist dies and is buried in the cemetery of the church Ognissanti in Florence.

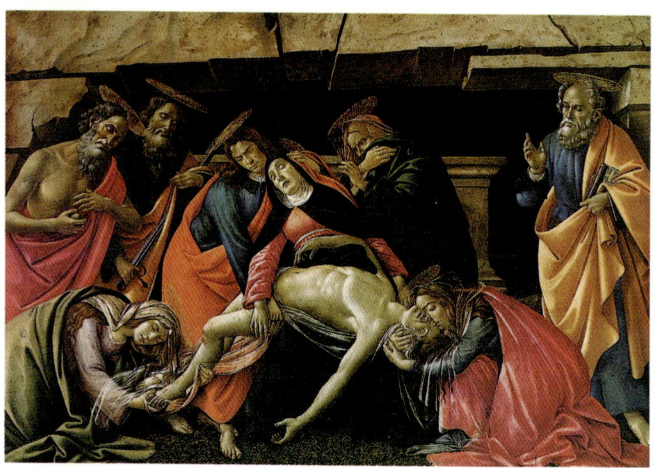

Above:
Pietà, c. 1490

Right:
The Mystic Nativity, c. 1501

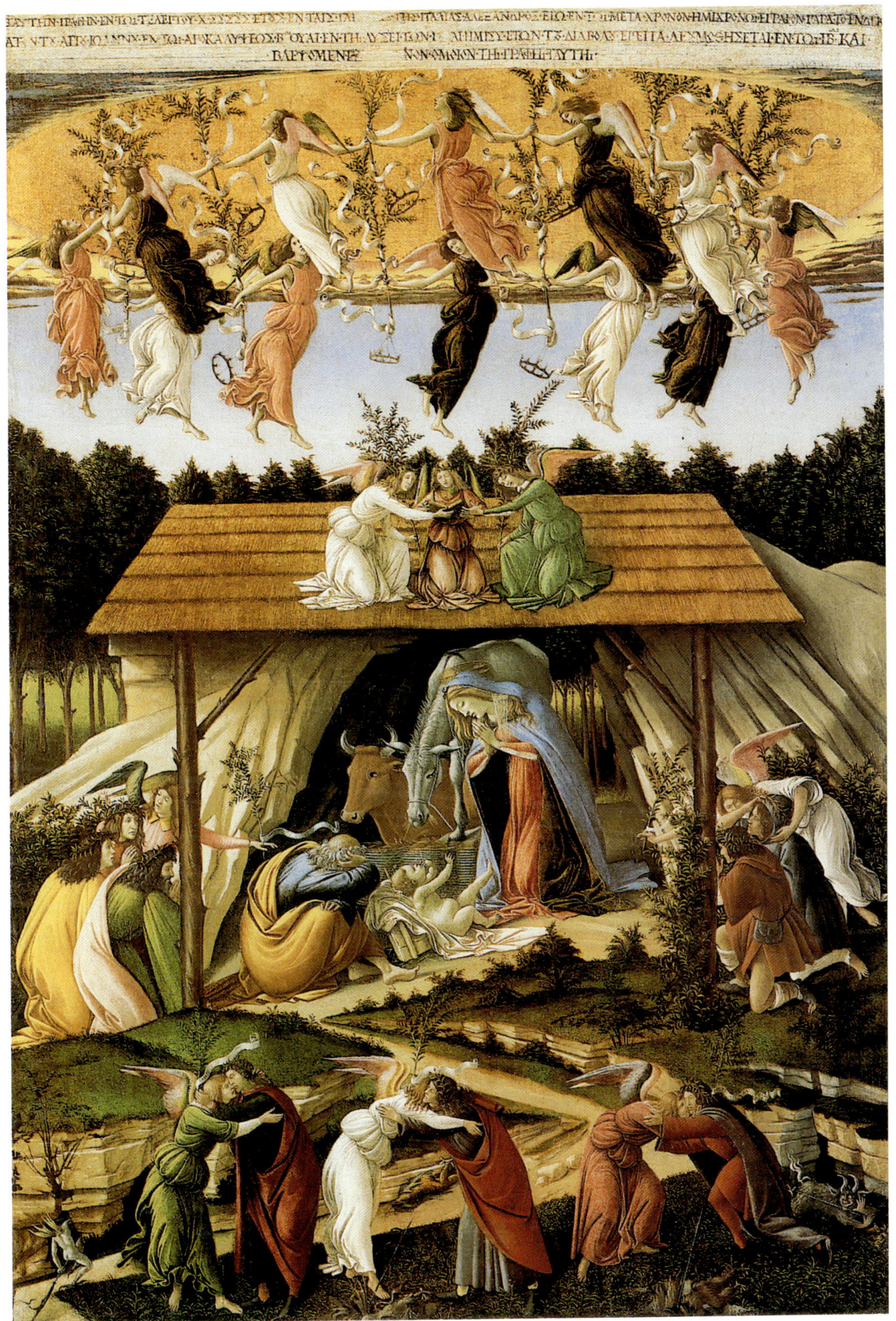

Notes

1 Herbert Horne, *Alessandro Filipepi Commonly Called Sandro Botticelli, Painter of Florence*, London 1908 (reprint, Florence 1986); Ronald Lightbown, *Sandro Botticelli: Life and Work*, 2 vols., London 1978; *The Dictionary of Art*, ed. Jane Turner, 34 vols., New York 1996, IV, pp. 493–504 (Charles Dempsey); Caterina Caneva, *Botticelli*, Florence 1990, and Barbara Deimling, *Botticelli*, Cologne 1993.

2 Benjamin Hederich, *Gründliches mythologisches Lexikon*, Leipzig 1770 (reprint, Darmstadt 1986); Wilhelm II. Roscher, *Ausführliches Lexikon der griechischen und römischen Mythologie*, 7 vols., Leipzig 1884ff; *Lexicon iconographicum mythologiae classicae*, Zurich 1981ff; Heinrich Krauss/Eva Uthemann, *Was Bilder erzählen*, Munich 1987; Jane Davidson Reid, *The Oxford Guide to Classical Mythology in the Arts, 1300–1990s*, 2 vols., New York/ Oxford 1993; Willem F. Lash, "Mythological Painting and Sculpture," in: *The Dictionary of Art*, XXII, pp. 410–417.

3 Karl Borinski, *Die Antike in Poetik und Kunsttheorie*, 2 vols., Leipzig 1914–1924; Erwin Panofsky, *Studies in Iconology*, New York 1962 (1st edition 1939); Jean Seznec, *The Survival of the Pagan Gods*, New York 1953; Edgar Wind, *Pagan Mysteries in the Renaissance*, Oxford 1980 (1st edition 1958); Erwin Panofsky, *Renaissance and Renascences in Western Art*, New York 1972 (1st edition 1960). The best overview in German is in the *Lexikon der christlichen Ikonographie*, ed. Engelbert Kirschbaum, 7 vols., Freiburg etc. 1970, II, pp. 170–179 (s.v. Götter, heidnische, by Wolfgang Kemp).

4 Ferrara, Palazzo Schifanoia, Salone dei Mesi, c. 1469–1476; Aby Warburg, "Kunst und internationale Astrologie im Palazzo Schifanoja zu Ferrara", in: *Atti del X congresso internazionale di storia dell'arte in Roma [1912]*, Rome 1922, repr. in: A. Warburg, *Ausgewählte Schriften und Würdigungen*, ed. D. Wuttke, Baden-Baden 1980, pp. 173–192; Eberhard Ruhmer, *Francesco del Cossa*, Munich 1959, pp. 71–75; Steffi Röttgen, *Wandmalerei der Frührenaissance in Italien*, 2 vols., Munich 1996–97, I, pp. 413–420.

5 Thus for example the Camera degli Sposi in Mantua, 1465–1475; Ronald Lightbown, *Mantegna*, Oxford 1986, p. 112 and pp. 415–419; Röttgen, *Wandmalerei*, II, pp.12–39.

6 Wind, *Pagan Mysteries*; Panofsky, *Renaissance.*

7 Ernst H. Gombrich, *Symbolic Images: Studies in the art of the Renaissance*, Oxford 1972, p. 45 (from: Marsilio Ficino, *Opera omnia*, Basel 1576, p. 807).

8 Lightbown, *Botticelli*, I, p. 93, II, pp. 55–56; Gombrich, *Symbolic Images*, pp. 66–69.

9 Roland Kecks, *Ghirlandaio*, Florence 1995, no. 15.

10 Giorgio Vasari, *Lives of the Most Eminent Painters, Sculptors and Architects*, translated by Gaston Du C. de Vere, 10 vols, London 1912–14, II, pp. 107–108. Author's note: The English translation of the Vasari text (like the translations by Mrs. Jonathan Foster and A. B. Hinds) does not take into account the art-historical use of the term *spalliera*, meaning decorative wall-panel, and refers here to "chair-backs"(the literal meaning of the word) which is clearly not appropriate in this context. The translation of *lettucio* as couch (instead of day bed) is also misleading. On the genre: Paul Schubring, *Cassoni: Truhen und Truhenbilder der italienischen Frührenaissance*, 2 vols., Leipzig 1915; Anne Brickey Barriault, *"Spalliera" Paintings of Renaissance Tuscany*, University Park (PA) 1994; Graham Hughes, *Renaissance Cassoni: Masterpieces of Early Italian Art: Painted Marriage Chests 1400–1550*, London 1997.

11 Krauss/ Uthemann, *Was Bilder erzählen*, pp. 37 and 41; Davidson Reid, *Classical Mythology*, II, pp. 966–976. To be precise, these four figures are satyr children; the terms faun and satyr have become interchangeable.

12 Ovid, *Ars amatoria*, 2.561–564; Lucretius, *De rerum natura*, 1.28–46; Horne, *Botticelli*, p. 141; Wind, *Pagan Mysteries*, pp. 89–92; Krauss/ Uthemann, *Was Bilder erzählen*, pp. 22–23; Davidson Reid, *Classical Mythology*, I, pp. 195–203.

13 Marsilio Ficino, *Commentary on the Symposium*, 5.8. (1339), cited in: Gombrich, *Symbolic Images*, p. 67.

14 Lucretius, *De rerum natura*, 1.31–37 in: *Lucretius De Rerum Natura*, with an English translation by W. H. D. Rouse, London and Cambridge, Mass. 1953, p. 5; Gombrich, *Symbolic Images*, pp. 66–69; Wind, *Pagan Mysteries*, p. 89.

15 Lucian, *Herodotos*, §5, cited in: Gombrich, *Symbolic Images*, p. 68.

16 Wind, *Pagan Mysteries*, pp. 89–92; Caneva, *Botticelli*, p. 83.

17 Lucian, *Herodotos*, §5, cited in: Gombrich, *Symbolic Images*, p. 68.

18 Lightbown, *Botticelli*, I, p. 93, II, pp. 55–56.

19 Rona Goffen, "Titian's *Sacred and Profane Love* and Marriage," in: N. Broude/ Mary Garrard (eds.), *The Expanding Discourse: Feminism and Art History*, New York 1992, pp. 111–125, partic. pp. 116–117; Christina Olsen, "Gross Expenditure: Botticelli's Nastagio degli

Onesti Panels," in: *Art History*, 15, 1992, pp. 146–170, partic. pp. 154–155; Rose Marie San Juan, "Mythology, Women and Renaissance Private Life: The Myth of Eurydice in Italian Furniture Painting," in: *Art History*, 15, 1992, pp. 127–145. Following also cited in note 23: Lilian Zirpolo, "Botticelli's *Primavera*: Lesson for a Bride," in: *women's art journal* 12, 1991/1992, pp. 24–26; Michael Rohlmann, "Botticellis *Primavera*: Zu Anlaß, Adressat und Funktion von mythologischen Gemälden im Florentiner Quattrocento," in: *Artibus et historiae*, 17, 1996.

20 Savonarola, "Sermon on the Book of Ruth," freely transl. from: Schubring, *Cassoni*, p. 380, and Edith Schaeffer, *Von Bildern und Menschen der Renaissance*, Berlin 1913, p. 8.

21 Vasari, *Lives*, III, p. 248; Aby Warburg, "Sandro Botticellis Geburt der Venus und Frühling," 1893, repr. in: A. Warburg, *Ausgewählte Schriften und Würdigungen*, pp. 11–64; Lightbown, *Botticelli*, II, cat. no. B39, partic. p. 52; Horne, *Botticelli*, pp. 49–62.

22 Charles Dempsey, *The Portrayal of Love: Botticelli's "Primavera" and Humanist Culture at the Time of Lorenzo the Magnificent*, Princeton 1992.

23 John Shearman, "The Collections of the Younger Branch of the Medici," in: *Burlington Magazine*, 117, 1975, pp. 12–27, p. 25, no. 38; Webster Smith, "On the Original Location of the *Primavera*," in: *Art Bulletin*, 57, 1975, pp. 31–40, p. 37, no. 9; Mirella Levi d'Ancona, *Botticelli's Primavera*, Florence 1983; Zirpolo, "Botticelli's *Primavera*," pp. 24–28; Rohlmann, "Botticellis *Primavera*," pp. 97–132; Frank Zöllner, "Zu den Quellen und zur Ikonographie von Botticellis *Primavera*," in: *Wiener Jahrbuch für Kunstgeschichte*, 50, 1997, pp. 131–157.

24 Ovid, *Metamorphoses*, 2.685–835, 8.618–727; Homer, *Iliad*, 24.334–469, *Odyssey*, 5.28–148; Krauss/ Uthemann, *Was Bilder erzählen*, pp. 26–27; Davidson Reid, *Classical Mythology*, I, pp. 563–572.

25 Lucius Apuleius, *The Golden Ass*, translated by W. Adlington, revised by S. Gaselee, London and Cambridge, Mass. 1915, 4.28–5.24, p. 191.

26 Columella, *De re rustica*, 10.192–214; Martianus Capella, *De nuptiis Mercurii et Philologiae libri*, 1.27, 9.888, and Remigius of Auxerre, *Commentum in Martianum Capellam*, ed. C. E. Lutz, Leiden 1962, p. 101 (Dempsey, *Portrayal of Love*, pp. 38 and 45–46; U. Rehm, [Review of Dempsey, *Portrayal of Love*], in: *Kunstchronik*, 47, 1994, pp. 96–104, p. 102).

27 Angelo Poliziano, *Stanze per la Giostra*, 1.40, cited in: Panofsky, *Renaissance*, p. 193

28 Cf. e.g. Angelo Poliziano, *Rusticus*, 210–221 (Dempsey, *Portrayal of Love*, pp. 20–49, partic. pp. 35–36).

29 Dempsey, *Portrayal of Love*, p. 38.

30 Zirpolo, "Botticelli's *Primavera*," p. 26; Cristelle L. Baskins, "Gender Trouble in Italian Renaissance Art History: Two Case Studies," in: *Studies in Iconography*, 16, 1994, pp. 1–36, pp. 2–16.

31 Barriault, *Spalliera-Paintings*, p. 28; Rohlmann, "Botticellis *Primavera*," pp. 102–104.

32 Cf. Susanne Kress, "Das autonome Porträt in Florenz," Phil. Diss., Gießen 1995, pp. 146–167.

33 Apuleius, *The Golden Ass*, 5.28, transl. by W. Adlington, pp. 241 and 243; Ovid, *Fasti*, 4.155–160; Giovanni Boccaccio, *Genealogia Deorum gentilium*, ed. Vincenzo Romano, Bari 1951, pp. 142–144 (3.22); Mirella Levi d'Ancona, *Botticelli's Primavera*, p. 50.

34 Mirella Levi d'Ancona, *The Garden of the Renaissance: Botanical Symbolism in Italian Painting*, Florence 1977, pp. 237–241, no. 3.

35 Rohlmann, "Botticellis *Primavera*"; Goffen, *Titian's "Sacred and Profane Love,"* p. 116.

36 Christina Olsen, "Gross Expenditure: Botticelli's Nastagio degli Onesti Panels," in: *Art History*, 15, 1992, pp. 146–170.

37 G. A. dell'Acqua/ R. Chiarelli, *L'opera completa del Pisanello*, Milan 1972, no. 115; Vicenzo Cartari, *Imagini delli Dei de gl'antichi*, Venice 1647 (Reprint, Graz 1963), pp. 54, 57, 60, 185 and 287.

38 Edmondo Solmi, "La festa del paradiso di Leonardo da Vinci e Bernardo Bellincioni," repr. in Solmi, *Scritti vinciani*, Florence 1976 (1st edn 1908), pp. 407–418, p. 418; Bernardo Bellincioni, *Le Rime*, ed. Pietro Fanfani, 2 vols., Bologna 1876–1878, II, p. 221.

39 Angelica Dülberg, *Privatporträts*, Berlin 1990, pp. 141–142; Frank Zöllner, *Leonardo da Vinci: Mona Lisa*, Frankfurt 1994, pp. 60–65.

40 Leon Battista Alberti, *The Family in Renaissance Florence*, a translation by Renée Neu Watkins of *I Libri della Famiglia*, Columbia 1969, pp. 115–116; Patricia Simons, "Women in Frames: The Gaze, the Eye, the Profile in Renaissance Portraiture," in: *History Workshop Journal*, 25, 1988, pp. 4–30, partic. p. 12.

41 "Sensa honestà perduta è la bellessa et sensa amor non fu mai gentilessa." This cassone may be seen in the Stibbert Museum in Florence; the inscription is cited by Paul Fraser Watson, *The Garden of Love in Tuscan Art of the Early Renaissance*, Philadelphia/ London 1979, p. 101.

42 Francis Ames-Lewis, "Early Medicean Devices," in: *Journal of the Warburg and Courtauld Institutes*, 42, 1979, pp. 128–129 and 142; Levi d'Ancona, *Botticelli's Primavera*, pp. 14, 42–43 and notes 53–54; Horst Bredekamp, *Sandro Botticelli: La Primavera*, Frankfurt 1988, pp. 50–54.

43 Ames-Lewis, "Early Medicean Devices," pp. 128–129 and 142; Mirella d'Ancona, *Due quadri del Botticelli eseguiti per nascità in casa Medici*, Florence 1992, pp. 22 and 56.

44 On the bridal chamber see John Kent Lydecker, *The Domestic Setting of the Arts in Renaissance Florence*, Ann Arbor 1987, pp. 170–175, on the purpose of sexual relations see Alberti, *I Libri della Famiglia*; Zirpolo, "Botticelli's *Primavera*," pp. 26–27.

45 Michael Baxandall, *Painting and Experience in Fifteenth-Century Italy*, Oxford/ New York 1988 (1st edn. 1972), pp. 29–108. On the following also see Zöllner, *Quellen und Ikonographie von Botticellis Primavera*.

46 Aby Warburg, *Bildniskunst und florentinisches Bürgertum I. Domenico Ghirlandajo in Santa Trinita. Die Bildnisse des Lorenzo de' Medici und seiner Angehörigen*, Leipzig n.d. [1902], partic. pp. 13–25; K. Langedijk, *The Portraits of the Medici 15th-18th Centuries*, 3 vols., Florence 1982, II, p. 1171, nos 74, 41 rev.

47 Zöllner, *Leonardo: Mona Lisa*, pp. 34, 54–55, colour plates, illus. 17, 31–32.

48 L. Stauch, *Reallexikon zur deutschen Kunstgeschichte*, II, s.v. Baum, pp. 63–73; Zöllner, *Quellen und Ikonographie von Botticellis Primavera*, pp. 146–151.

49 *Speculum Virginum*, Leipzig, University Library; A. Katzenellenbogen, Allegories of the Virtues and Vices in Medieval Art, New York 1964 (1st edn. London 1939), pp. 65–68 and illus. 64–68; G. B. Ladner, "Vegetation Symbolism and the Concept of Renaissance," in: *De artibus opuscula XL. Essays in Honour of Erwin Panofsky*, ed. M. Meiss, 2 vols, New York 1960, I, pp. 303–322, pp. 308–312.

50 Levi d'Ancona, *Garden of the Renaissance*, pp. 272–277, 208–209 and 381–387.

51 H. Wohl, *The Paintings of Domenico Veneziano ca. 1410–1461*, Oxford 1980, pp. 32–63 and cat. no. 5.

52 Peter Humfrey, *Cima da Conegliano*, Cambridge etc. 1983, cat. no. 145.

53 Levi d'Ancona, *Botticelli's Primavera*, pp. 15 and 25–27; Rohlmann, "Botticellis *Primavera*," pp. 126–127.

54 Lightbown, *Botticelli*, II, no. B43; Zirpolo, "Botticelli's *Primavera*"; Rohlmann, "Botticellis *Primavera*," pp. 118–119.

55 Transl. from: Hans Liebeschütz, *Fulgentius Metaphoralis*, Leipzig/ Berlin 1926 (*Studien der Bibliothek Warburg* IV), p. 124; Rudolf Wittkower, *Allegorie und der Wandel der Symbole in Antike und Renaissance*, Cologne 1983 (1st English edition 1937/1938), p. 401, note 34.

56 Ibid., partic. pp. 257–263.

57 *"Le temps revient," 'L Tempo si rinuova: Feste e spettacoli nella Firenze di Lorenzo il Magnifico*, ed. Paola Ventrone, Florence 1992, p. 39; Cecilia De Carli, *I deschi da parto e la pittura del primo Rinascimento toscano*, Turin 1997, no. 39; Anne Jacobsen-Schutte, "Trionfo delle donne: tematiche di rovesciamento dei ruoli della Firenze rinascimentale," in: *Quaderni storici*, 44, 1980, pp. 474–496.

58 The Bible, Book of Judges, 16; Kraus/ Uthemann, *Was Bilder erzählen*, pp. 164–165 and 221.

59 Horst W. Janson, *Donatello*, 2 vols., Princeton 1957, I, pp. 200–204; Volker Herzner, "Die 'Judith' der Medici," in: *Zeitschrift für Kunstgeschichte*, 43, 1980, pp. 139–180; John Pope-Hennessy, *Italian Renaissance Sculpture*, 4th edition, London 1996, pp. 359–360.

60 Ames-Lewis, *Early Medicean Devices*; Patricia Simons, "Women in Frames," in: *History Workshop Journal*, 25, 1988, pp. 4–30, partic. pp. 9–13; Kress, *Das autonome Porträt in Florenz*.

61 Leon Battista Alberti, "De re aedificatoria," 9.4 in: *On the Art of Building in Ten Books*, transl. by Joseph Rykwert, Neil Leach and Robert Tavernor, Cambridge, Mass. and London 1988, p. 299.

62 Warburg, *Botticellis Geburt der Venus und Frühling*; Horne, *Botticelli*, pp. 148–153; Wind, *Pagan Mysteries*, pp. 128–140 and pp. 263–264; Lightbown, *Botticelli*, I, pp. 86–90, and II, pp. 64–65; Levi d'Ancona, *Due Quadri del Botticelli*, pp. 51–62.

63 On flower symbolism: Levi d'Ancona, *Garden of the Renaissance*, pp. 113–114 (cornflowers) and 124–126 (daisies).

64 Hesiod, *Theogony*, 174–201, partic. 194–195.

65 Homer, "To Aphrodite," in: *The Homeric Hymns*, ed. Apostolos N. Athanassakis, Baltimore and London 1976, p. 55.

66 Tibullus, *Carmina*, 3.3.34; Wind, *Pagan Mysteries*, p. 263; Guy de Tervarent, *Attributs et symboles dans l'art profane 1450–1600*, 2 vols., Geneva 1958, I, p. 114; Manfred Lurker, *Wörterbuch der Symbolik*, 5th edition, Stuttgart 1991, pp. 496–497; Piera Bocci Pacini, "Nota archeologica sulla nascita di Venere," in: *Gli Uffizi. Studi e ricerche*, 4, Florence 1987, pp. 19–32.

67 "E dentro nata in acti uaghi et lieti, Una donzella non con human uolto, Da zephiri lasciui spinta a proda, Gir soura un Nichio; et par chel ciel ne goda." Angelo Poliziano, *Stanze per la Giostra*, 1.99.5–9, cited in: Horne, *Botticelli*, p. 149.

68 "Giurar potresti che dellonde uscissi La Dea premendo colla dextra il crino, Collaltra il dolce pomo ricoprissi." Poliziano, *Stanze per la Giostra*, 1.101.1–3, cited in: Horne, *Botticelli*, p. 149.
69 *Benvenuti de Rimbaldis de Imola Comentum super Dantis Aldigherij Comoediam*, ed. J. P. Lacaita, 5 vols., Florence 1887, III, pp. 279–280, p. 280; Frank Zöllner, "'Policretior manu' – Zum Polykletbild der frühen Neuzeit," in: *Polyklet*, exh. cat., Liebieg Haus, Frankfurt 1990, pp. 450–472, p. 458.
70 Wind, *Pagan Mysteries*, 132.
71 Günter Passavant, *Verrocchio als Maler*, Düsseldorf, 1959, pp. 58–87; Gombrich, *Symbolic Images*, p. 91.
72 Hesiod, *Theogony*, pp. 173–200; Anacreon, *Odes*, p. 51; Wind, *Pagan Mysteries*, pp. 133–136; Levi d'Ancona, *Garden of the Renaissance*, pp. 330.
73 Pliny, *Historia naturalis*, 21.94.165, cited in: Levi d'Ancona, *Garden of the Renaissance*, p. 44.
74 "Nel tempestoso Egeo in grembo a Tethi, Si uede il fusto genitale accolto." Poliziano, *Stanze per la Giostra*, 1.99.1–2, cited in: Horne, *Botticelli*, p. 149.
75 Horace, *Satires*, 1.8.3–6.
76 Kenneth Clark, *Leonardo da Vinci*, 2nd edition, Harmondsworth 1958, p. 116; *Leonardo da Vinci*, exh. cat., Hayward Gallery, ed. M. Kemp and J. Roberts, London 1989, p. 38 and no. 14.
77 Hyginus, *Astronomia*, 2.8; Hederich, *Mythologisches Lexikon*, col. 1446–1448; Davidson Reid, *Classical Mythology*, II, pp. 629–35.
78 Levi d'Ancona, *Due Quadri del Botticelli*, pp. 51–62.
79 Horne, *Botticelli*, pp. 144–148; Lightbown, *Botticelli*, I, p. 96, II, pp. 60–63; Susanne Kress, "Die 'Camera di Lorenzo, bella' im Palazzo Tornabuoni," in: *Mitteilungen des Kunsthistorischen Instituts in Florenz*, 42, 1997 (in preparation).
80 Everett Fahy, "The Tornabuoni-Albizzi Panels," in: *Scritti di storia dell'arte in onore di Federico Zeri*, 2 vols., Milan 1984, I, pp. 233–247; Kress, "Camera di Lorenzo."
81 Martianus Capella, *De nuptiis Philologiae et Mercurii*, books 3–9. On the moral aspect cf. the sonnet by Burchiello, cited by Horne, *Botticelli*, p. 145
82 "Septe son l'arti liberali: & prima Grammatica dell'altre e uia & porta." Burchiello, ibid.
83 Andrea di Bonaiuto, *Triumph of St. Thomas Aquinas*, circa 1366–68, Florence, Santa Maria Novella.
84 Capella, *De nuptiis Philologiae et Mercurii*, books 1–2; Veronica Mertens, *Die drei Grazien*, Wiesbaden 1994, pp. 190–194.

Select Bibliography

My interpretations of Sandro Botticelli's mythological paintings are based on older iconological research and on monographic studies (see Notes) as well as on the findings of more recent research into the Renaissance, which may be summarized as follows: In the fifteenth century, private patrons commissioned works with profane themes above all to decorate their own residences in an elevated manner. As a rule these works commemorated specific events, most notably weddings, but also births, the coming of age, new homes, and death. In keeping with this, most of Botticelli's profane paintings and some of his religious panel paintings can be traced back to occasions of this kind.

Barriault, Anne B. *"Spalliere" Paintings of Renaissance Tuscany*. University Park, PA: 1994.

Baskins, Cristelle L. "*La festa di Susanna*: Virtue on Trial in Renaissance Sacred Drama and Painted Wedding Chests." In *Art History* 14 (1991): 329–344.

———. "Griselda or the Renaissance Bride Stripped Bare by Her Bachelor in Tuscan Cassone Painting." In *Stanford Italian Review* 10 (1991): 153–175.

———. "Gender trouble in Italian Renaissance History: Two Case Studies." In *Studies in Iconography* 16 (1994): 1–36.

Bischoff, Uwe. *Die "Cassonebilder" des Piero di Cosimo: Fragen der Ikonographie*. Frankfurt: 1995.

Braham, Allan. "The Bed of Pierfrancesco Borgherini." In

Burlington Magazine 121 (1979): 754–765.

Callmann, Ellen. *Apollonio di Giovanni.* Oxford: 1974.

———. "An Apollonio di Giovanni for an Historic Marriage." In *Burlington Magazine* 119 (1977): 174–181.

———. "The Growing Threat to Marital Bliss as Seen in Fifteenth-century Florentine Paintings." In *Studies in Iconography* 5 (1979): 73–92.

———. "Botticelli's Life of Saint Zenobius." In *Art Bulletin* 66 (1984): 492–496.

———. "Apollonio di Giovanni and Painting for the Early Renaissance Room." In *Antichità viva* 27, 3–4 (1988): 5–18

Christiansen, Keith. "Lorenzo Lotto and the Tradition of Epithalamic Paintings." In *Apollo* 124 (1986): 166–173.

Cole Ahl, Diane. "Renaissance Birth Salvers and the Richmond *Judgement of Solomon.*" In *Studies in Iconography* 7–8 (1981–1982): 157–174.

De Carli, Cecilia. *I deschi da parto e la pittura del primo Rinascimento toscano.* Turin: 1997.

Diefendorf, Barbara B. "Family Culture, Renaissance Culture." In *Renaissance Quarterly* 40 (1987): 661–681

Fahy, Everett. "The Tornabuoni-Albizzi Panel." In *Scritti di storia dell'arte in onore di Federico Zeri.* 2 vols. Milan: 1984. 1: 233–247.

Goffen, Rona. "Renaissance Dreams." In *Renaissance Quarterly* 40 (1987): 682–706, 752–761.

———. "Titian's *Sacred and Profane Love* and Marriage." In *The Expanding Discourse. Feminism and Art History,* edited by N. Broude/Mary Garrard, 111–125. New York: 1992.

Hall, Marietta van. "Messer Marsiglio and His Bride." In *Connoisseur* 192 (1976): 292–297.

Hansmann, Martina. *Andrea del Castagnos Zyklus der "uomini famosi" und "donne famose": Geschichtsverständnis und Tugendideal in florentinischen Frühhumanismus.* Münster/Hamburg: 1993.

Hayum, A. "Michelangelo's *Doni Tondo*: Holy Family and Family Myth." In *Studies in Iconography* 8 (1981–82): 209–251.

Hughes, Graham. *Renaissance Cassone Masterpieces of Early Italian Art: Painted Marriage Chests 1400–1550.* London: 1997.

Klapisch-Zuber, Christiane. *Das Haus, der Name, der Brautschatz. Strategien und Rituale im gesellschlaftlichen Leben der Renaissance.* Frankfurt (Main)/New York: 1995.

Königer, Maribel. "Die profanen Fresken des Palazzo Davanzatti in Florenz. Private Repräsentation zur Zeit der internationalen Gotik." In *Mitteilungen des Kunsthistorischen Instituts in Florenz* 34 (1990): 245–278.

Kress, Susanne. "Das autonome Porträt in Florenz: Studien zu Ort, Funktion und Entwicklung des florentinischen Bildnisses im Quattrocento." Ph.D. diss., Gießen, 1995.

Lydecker, John Kent. *The Domestic Setting of the Arts in Renaissance Florence.* Ann Arbor: 1987.

Lynch, Peter F. "Narratives of Marginalization: De-Centering Women in Tuscan Domestic Painting ca. 1500." In *Studies in -Iconography* 16 (1994): 139–164.

Marek, Michaela. "Raffaels Loggia di. Psiche in der Farnesina: Überlegungen zu Rekonstruktion und Deutung." In *Jahrbuch der Berliner Museen* 26 (1984): 257–290.

Olsen, Christina. "Gross Expenditure: Botticelli's Nastagio degli Onesti Panels." In *Art History* 15 (1992): 146–170.

Ost, Hans. "Tizians *Himmlische und Irdische Liebe.*" In *Wallraf-Richartz-Jahrbuch* 12 (1980): 87–104.

Owen Hughes, Diane. "Representing the Family: Portraits and Purposes in Early Modern Italy." In *Journal of Interdisciplinary History* 27 (1986): 7–38

Pons, Nicoletta. "Il 'Tempio in Casa:' immagini, allegorie, mobili 'scortati'." In *Maestri e botteghe. Pittura a Firenze alle fine del Quattrocento,* edited by M. Gregori et al., 219–231. Milan: 1992.

Pope-Hennessy, John, and Keith Christiansen. *Secular Painting in 15th-Century Tuscany: Birth Trays, Cassone Panels, and Portraits.* New York: 1980. First published in *Metropolitan Museum of Art Bulletin* (Summer 1980).

Rohlmann, Michael. "Botticellis *Primavera*: Zu Anlaß, Adressat und Funktion von mythologischen Gemälden im Florentiner Quattrocento." In *Artibus et historiae* 17 (1996): 96–132.

San Juan, Rose Marie. "Mythology, Women and Renaissance Private Life: The Myth of Eurydice in Italian Furniture Painting." In *Art History* 15 (1992): 127–145

Schiapiarelli, Attilo. *La casa fiorentina e i suoi arredi nei secoli XIV e XV,* edited by M. Sframeli. 2 vols. Florence: 1983. First published in 1908.

Thornton, Peter. *The Italian Renaissance Interior 1400–1600.* London: 1991.

Watson, Paul Fraser. *"Virtù" and "voluptas" in Cassone Painting.* Ann Arbor: 1974.

———. *The Garden of Love in Tuscan Art of the Early Renaissance.* Philadelphia/London: 1979.

Witthoft, Brucia. "Marriage Rituals and Marriage Chests in Quattrocento Florence." In *Artibus et Historiae* 5 (1982): 43–59.

Zirpolo, Lilian. "Botticelli's *Primavera*: Lesson for a Bride." In *women's art journal* 12 (1991/1992): 24–28.

Zöllner, Frank. "Leonardo's Portrait of Mona Lisa del Giocondo." In *Gazette des Beaux-Arts* 121 (1993): 115–138.

———. *Leonardo da Vinci. Mona Lisa.* Frankfurt: 1994.

Photography Credits

La Scala, Istituto Fotographico, Florence: pp. 20–21, 32–33, 68, 80–81 (including all details)

Agence photographique de la réunion des musées nationaux, Paris: pp. 100, 106 (including all details)

National Gallery, London: pp. 12–13 (including all details)

University of Leipzig, Institut für Kunstgeschichte, Photothek: pp. 24, 26, 50, 53, 59, 66, 74, 97

Archive of the author: pp. 46, 49, 52, 58

All other photographs are from the archive of the publisher.

List of Illustrations

Main essay:
Works by Sandro Botticelli

pp. 12/13
Mars and Venus, 1483
Tempera on wood
27 ¼ x 68 ¼ in. (69 x 173.5 cm)
The National Gallery, London

pp. 32/33
La Primavera, c. 1482
Tempera on poplar
80 x 123 ½ in. (203 x 314 cm)
Uffizi Gallery, Florence

p. 68
Minerva and the Centaur, c. 1482–83
Egg tempera and oil on canvas
81 ½ x 58 ¼ in. (207 x 148 cm)
Uffizi Gallery, Florence

pp. 80/81
The Birth of Venus (The Arrival of Venus)
c. 1484–86
Tempera on canvas
69 x 109 ½ in. (172.5 x 278.5 cm)
Uffizi Gallery, Florence

p. 100
Lorenzo Tornabuoni Presented to the Liberal Arts, c. 1488
Fresco transferred onto canvas
93 ¾ x 111 ¾ in. (238 x 284 cm)
Musée du Louvre, Paris

p. 106
Giovanna Albizzi, Venus and the Three Graces, c. 1488
Fresco transferred onto canvas
83 x 111 ¾ in. (211 x 284 cm)
Musée du Louvre, Paris

Illustrations for Comparison

p. 15
Domenico Ghirlandaio (1449–1494)
The Birth of Mary, c. 1485–90
Fresco
Main choir chapel,
Santa Maria Novella, Florence

p. 24
Sarcophagus with Bacchus and Ariadne (detail)
Vatican Museum, Rome

p. 26
Coat of arms of the Vespucci family

p. 46
Italian, late 15th century
Portrait Medallion of Lorenzo di Pierfrancesco de' Medici
(recto)

p. 47
Sandro Botticelli
Portrait of a Man with a Medal of Cosimo the Elder, c. 1475
Tempera on wood
22 ½ x 17 ¼ in. (57.5 x 44 cm)
Uffizi Gallery, Florence

p. 49
Antonio Pisanello (1395–1455)
Portrait Medallion of Cecilia Gonzaga
(verso)

p. 50
Drawing of the Three Graces from the *Codex Coburgensis*, c. 1550
Veste Coburg

p. 52
Niccolò Fiorentino, attributed to (1430–1514)
Portrait Medallion of Giovanna Albizzi
(verso), c. 1486

p. 53
Woodcut from *Questo sia la nobilissima historia di Maria per Ravenna* (The most noble history of Mary for Ravenna), c. 1480

p. 58
Niccolò Fiorentino, attributed to (1430–1514)
Portrait Medallion of Lorenzo il Magnifico
(verso)

p. 59
Tree of virtues from the *Speculum Virginum*, (late 14th century)
University Library, Leipzig
(Mss. 665, fol. 40)

p.61
Domenico Veneziano (d. 1461)
Madonna and Child with Saints, c. 1445
(Altarpiece for Santa Lucia de' Magnoli)
Tempera on wood
82 ¼ x 85 in. (209 x 216 cm)
Uffizi Gallery, Florence

p. 62
Cima da Conegliano
(1459/60–1517/18)
Madonna and Child with Saints (Madonna dell'Arancio), c. 1496
Oil on wood, 83 ½ x 54 ¾
(212 x 139 cm)
The Academy, Venice

p. 66
Woodcut from Jacobus de Cessoli's *Libro di giuocho degli scacchi* (Book on the game of chess), 1493/94

p. 74
Workshop of Apollonio di Giovanni
Triumph of Love
Birth salver
Diameter 21 ½ in. (55 cm)
Victoria & Albert Museum, London

p. 75
Donatello (1386–1466)
Judith and Holofernes, c. 1456
Bronze
H. 93 in. (236 cm)
Palazzo Vecchio, Florence

p. 86
Cameo with Venus in the Shell
Antiquarium, Berlin

p. 90
Roman (copy of a Greek original from the early 3rd century B.C.)
Medici Venus, c. 1st century B.C.
Marble
H. 60 ¼ in. (153 cm)
Uffizi Gallery, Florence

p. 91
Giovanni Pisano (d. after 1314)
Temperantia (Moderation), 1302–1312
Marble
Detail of pulpit, Cathedral of Pisa

p. 92
Andrea del Verrocchio (c. 1435–1488) and Leonardo da Vinci (1452–1519)
The Baptism of Christ, c. 1470–75
Tempera and oil on wood
69 ¾ x 59 ½ in. (177 x 151 cm)
Uffizi Gallery, Florence

p. 96
Cesar de Sesto, attributed to
Leda and the Swan
38 x 29 in. (96.5 x 73.7 cm)
Collection of the Earl of Pembroke and Wilton House Trust, Salisbury, England

p. 97
Leonardo da Vinci (1452–1519)
Leda and the Swan
Windsor Castle, England
(Nr. 12430v)

Biography of the Artist: Works by Sandro Botticelli

p. 115
La Fortezza (Fortitude), c. 1470
Tempera on wood
65 ¾ x 73 ½ in. (167 x 87 cm)
Uffizi Gallery, Florence

p. 116
St. Sebastian, c. 1473
Tempera on wood
76 ¾ x 29 ½ in. (195 x 75 cm)
Gemäldegalerie, Staatliche Museen zu Berlin Preussischer Kulturbesitz, Berlin

St. Augustine, 1480
Fresco
72 ¾ x 48 ½ in. (185 x 123 cm)
Ognissanti, Florence

p. 117
Adoration of the Magi (The Lama Adoration), c. 1475–76
Tempera on wood
43 ¾ x 52 ¾ in. (111 x 134 cm)
Uffizi Gallery, Florence

Portrait of Giuliano de' Medici, 1476–78
Tempera on wood
30 x 20 ¾ in. (76 x 52.6 cm)
The National Gallery of Art, Washington, D.C.

p. 118
Madonna and Child with SS. John the Baptist and John the Evangelist (Bardi Altarpiece), 1484–85
Poplar
72 ¾ x 71 in. (185 x 180 cm)
Gemäldegalerie, Staatliche Museen zu Berlin Preussischer Kulturbesitz, Berlin

p. 119
La Calunnia (The Calumny of Apelles), c. 1494–95
Tempera on wood
24 ½ x 35 ¾ in. (62 x 91 cm)
Uffizi Gallery, Florence

p. 120
Pietà, c. 1490
Tempera on wood
55 x 81 ½ in. (140 x 207 cm)
Alte Pinakothek, Munich

p. 121
The Mystic Nativity, c. 1501
Tempera on canvas
42 ¾ x 29 ½ in. (108.5 x 75 cm)
The National Gallery, London